PIERRE CHAREAU

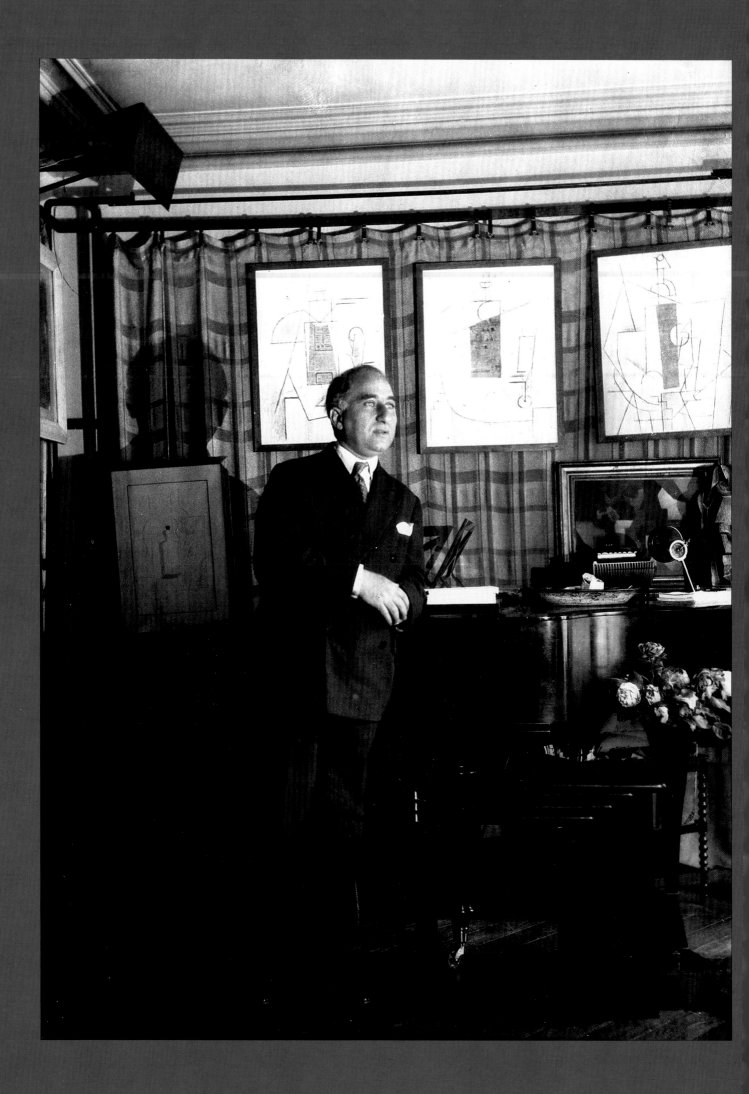

PIERRE CHAREAU

DESIGNER AND ARCHITECT

BRIAN BRACE TAYLOR

BENEDIKT TASCHEN

PREMIERE PAGE DE COUVERTURE:
Détail de la salle de séjour, Maison de Verre.
DOS DE COUVERTURE:
Voir repr. p. 62, 68, 73, 76/77, 122/123
PAGE DE GARDE:
Dessin de Chareau sur le dos d'une enveloppe.
FRONTISPICE:
Pierre Chareau dans son appartement à Paris,
vers 1927.

FRONT COVER:
Detail of the living room in the Maison de Verre.
BACK COVER:
Cf. ill. pp. 62, 68, 73, 76/77, 122/123
FLY TITLE:
Drawing by Chareau on the back of an
envelope.
FRONTISPIECE:
Pierre Chareau in his Paris apartment, c. 1927.

UMSCHLAGVORDERSEITE:
Detail des Wohnzimmers in der Maison de
Vorro.
UMSCHLAGRÜCKSEITE:
Siehe Abb. S. 62, 68, 73, 76/77, 122/123
SCHMUTZTITEL:
Zeichnung von Chareau auf der Rückseite eines
Briefumschlags.
FRONTISPIZ:
Pierre Chareau in seinem Pariser Apartment,
um 1927.

© 1992 Benedikt Taschen Verlag GmbH
Hohenzollernring 53, D-5000 Köln 1
Edited and designed by Peter Feierabend, Berlin
Coedited by Sally Bald, Cologne
French translation: Marie-Anne Trémeau-Böhm, Cologne
German translation: Stephanie Giltjes, Cologne
Colour reproductions: ReproColor, Bocholt
Black and white reproductions: Reproservice Pees, Essen
Printed in Germany
ISBN 3-8228-9341-2

Sommaire

Contents

Inhalt

Préface

Le fait que Pierre Chareau reste pratiquement inconnu du grand public aussi bien dans son pays natal, la France, qu'à l'étranger, et représente malgré tout un nom fort respecté – voire vénéré – dans le monde des arts décoratifs et du mouvement moderne en architecture, est un paradoxe. Bien que le chef d'œuvre de Chareau, la Maison Dalsace – connue sous le nom de Maison de Verre –, ait été largement diffusé dans la presse populaire de l'époque, il fut oublié par la suite. Les revues d'architecture des années trente attachées aux tendances avant-gardistes, comme «L'Architecture d'Aujourd'hui» en France et «OPBOUW» en Hollande, publièrent des articles sur la maison achevée pour n'y revenir que rarement, sauf de temps à autre sous forme de photographie illustrant une publicité ou un thème. Pourquoi Chareau, le designer et ensemblier, l'architecte et proche compagnon de tant de grands peintres, sculpteurs, compositeurs et critiques des années vingt et trente, glissa-t-il dans l'obscurité pendant presque trente ans? Pourquoi, de plus, son œuvre attire-t-elle maintenant l'attention d'éminents architectes et historiens contemporains? Les contributions apportées par Chareau au monde du meuble et du design étaient-elles vraiment en marge du courant dominant, et sa Maison Dalsace était-elle simplement une curiosité? Comment expliquer le fait qu'il ait été redécouvert à la fin des années soixante, que les meubles conçus par lui aient atteint des prix excessifs dans les années quatre-vingt et que sa Maison de Verre soit pratiquement devenue un lieu de pélerinage des designers modernes?

Preface

It is a paradoxical fact that Pierre Chareau remains virtually unknown to the general public both inside and outside his native France, and yet represents a highly-respected – indeed, almost venerated – name in the world of the decorative arts and the Modern Movement in architecture. Although the *chef-d'œuvre* of Chareau's creative career, the Dalsace House – known as the Maison de Verre (glass house) – received wide coverage in the popular press of the day, it was subsequently forgotten. The architectural magazines of the mid–1930s devoted to avant-garde trends, such as »L'Architecture d'Aujourd'hui« in France and »OPBOUW« in Holland, carried articles on the completed house, only rarely to return to it again, unless in the occasional form of a photograph illustrating an advertisement or a theme. Why did Chareau the furniture designer and interior decorator, the architect and close companion of so many of the great painters, sculptors, composers and critics of the 1920s and '30s, slip into obscurity for nearly thirty years? Why, too, is his work now attracting the attention of the eminent architects and historians of our day? Were Chareau's contributions to the world of furniture and interior design really only marginal to the mainstream, and was his Dalsace house just a freak curiosity? How should we explain his rediscovery in the late 1960s, the exceedingly high prices commanded by his furniture designs in the 1980s, and the fact that his Maison de Verre has become a virtual Mecca for modern-day designers?

Einführung

Es ist schon paradox, daß Pierre Chareau der breiten Öffentlichkeit sowohl in seiner Heimat Frankreich als auch im Ausland eigentlich unbekannt geblieben ist, und das, obwohl sein Name in der Welt der dekorativen Künste und der Modernen Architekturbewegung hoch angesehen, ja regelrecht verehrt wird. Das »Chef d'œuvre« in Chareaus kreativer Laufbahn, das Dalsace Haus – bekannt als Maison de Verre (Glashaus) –, wurde zwar in der allgemeinen Tagespresse erschöpfend behandelt, dann aber alsbald wieder vergessen. Die Architekturmagazine Mitte der dreißiger Jahre, die sich den avantgardistischen Trends widmeten, wie z. B. »L'Architecture d'Aujourd'hui« in Frankreich oder »OPBOUW« in den Niederlanden, berichteten über das fertiggestellte Haus und kamen nur selten wieder darauf zurück, und wenn, dann nur in Form von gelegentlichen Fotografien, die der Illustration eines Inserates oder Themas dienten. Warum geriet Chareau, der Möbeldesigner und Innenarchitekt, der Architekt und vertraute Gefährte so vieler großer Maler, Bildhauer, Komponisten und Kritiker der zwanziger und dreißiger Jahre dieses Jahrhunderts, für beinahe dreißig Jahre in Vergessenheit? Und aus welchem Grund zieht sein Werk gegenwärtig die Aufmerksamkeit der bedeutendsten Architekten und Historiker unserer Tage auf sich? Standen Chareaus Beiträge in der Welt des Möbeldesigns und der Innenarchitektur wirklich nur am Rande der Hauptströmung, und war sein Haus für die Dalsaces lediglich eine Kuriosität? Wie lassen sich seine Wiederentdeckung in den späten sechziger Jahren, die außerordentlich hohen Preise, die seine Möbelentwürfe in den achtziger Jahren erzielten, und die Tatsache, daß seine Maison de Verre praktisch zu einem Mekka für heutige Designer geworden ist, erklären?

Sa vie

L'énigme de l'œuvre de Chareau est, du moins en partie, un reflet de notre manque d'information au sujet de son histoire, de sa philosophie, de sa manière de travailler, de sa personnalité et de ses objectifs professionnels. C'est seulement depuis 1984 et la première tentative faite pour créer un «catalogue raisonné» complet de ses meubles que nous avons commencé à comprendre plus clairement et plus profondément l'importance de Chareau.[1]

Contrairement à Le Corbusier ou à l'architecte américain Frank Lloyd Wright, qui écrivirent et publièrent de nombreux ouvrages à propos de leurs idées et d'eux-mêmes, Pierre Chareau ne nous a guère laissé de déclarations personnelles. Nous sommes obligés de nous fier à son entourage, en commençant par sa femme Dollie qui a laissé des lettres et des récits relatifs aux quarante-six années qu'ils passèrent ensemble. L'information est relativement maigre, souvent anecdotique, et le plus fréquemment sans rapport avec sa vie professionnelle. Il a seulement publié quelques articles.

Ce que nous savons est que Pierre Paul Constant Chareau est né le 3 août 1883 à Bordeaux et qu'il était le fils d'Ester Carvallo et d'Adolphe Chareau. Son père était à l'origine «négociant en vins», mais perdit sa fortune et alla s'installer à Paris où il travailla dans les chemins de fer. Chareau avait une sœur.

D'après ses propres dires, Dollie (née Louise Dyte) rencontra son futur mari alors qu'il avait seize ans et elle dix-neuf; ils se marièrent cinq ans plus tard, en 1904. Ils n'eurent pas d'enfants. Comme elle était née et avait grandi en Angleterre, Dollie Chareau gagna de l'argent au début de leur vie commune en donnant des leçons d'anglais, tandis que Pierre travaillait dans les bureaux parisiens de Waring & Gillow, une grande compagnie britannique spécialisée dans les meubles et le design. Il entra dans la firme en 1899 ou 1900 comme dessinateur et la quitta en avril 1914 comme maître dessinateur.

Les études suivies par Pierre Chareau après le lycée restent obscures. On n'a pas la preuve que Chareau a régulièrement fréquenté une école d'architecture parisienne en tant qu'étudiant. Selon le système alors

His Life

The enigma of Chareau's work is at least in part a reflection of our lack of information about the man's history, philosophy and manner of working, his personality and his professional objectives. Only since 1984 and the first attempt to assemble an exhaustive »catalogue raisonné« of his furniture have we begun to formulate a somewhat clearer, deeper understanding of Chareau's greatness.[1]

Unlike Le Corbusier or the American architect Frank Lloyd Wright, both of whom wrote and published a great deal about their ideas and themselves, Pierre Chareau bequeathed little in the way of personal testimony. We are obliged to rely on the family and friends who knew him, beginning with his wife Dollie, who has left letters and accounts of their life of forty-six years together. The information is relatively sparse, often anecdotal, and mostly unrelated to his professional life. He published only a few articles.

What we do know is that Pierre Paul Constant Chareau was born on 3 August 1883 in Bordeaux to Ester Carvallo and Adolphe Chareau. His father was a wine merchant (»négociant«) originally, but lost his fortune and moved to Paris where he worked on the railroads. He had one sister.

By her own account, Dollie (born Louise Dyte) met her future husband when he was sixteen years old, and she nineteen; they married five years later in 1904. They had no children. Born and raised in England, Dollie Chareau earned money during their early life together by giving English lessons, while Pierre worked in the Paris offices of Waring & Gillow, a large British company specializing in furniture and interior design. He joined the firm in 1899 or 1900 as a tracing draughtsman, and left in April 1914 having risen to the rank of master draughtsman.

Pierre Chareau's education beyond secondary school remains obscure. No evidence has yet come to light that Chareau attended a school of architecture in Paris as a regular student. According to the Beaux Arts system of the time, however, he could easily have followed courses in one of the ateliers without having to pass the entrance exams to register formally; he may well have done this in the evenings after

Sein Leben

Das Rätsel um Chareaus Werk reflektiert zumindest teilweise unseren Mangel an Informationen, sowohl über den Werdegang, die Lebensphilosophie und Arbeitsweise des Mannes als auch über seine Persönlichkeit und seine beruflichen Ziele. Erst seit 1984 der erste Versuch unternommen wurde, einen umfassenden »catalogue raisonné« seiner Möbel zu erstellen, haben wir begonnen, die Bedeutung Chareaus besser zu verstehen und sie in Worte zu fassen.[1] Anders als Le Corbusier oder der amerikanische Architekt Frank Lloyd Wright, die beide sehr viel über sich selbst und über ihre Ideen schrieben und veröffentlichten, hinterließ Pierre Chareau nur wenig Aufschlußreiches über seine Person. Wir müssen uns also auf die Aussagen seiner Familie und Freunde stützen, angefangen bei seiner Frau Dollie, die Briefe und Berichte aus ihrer sechsundvierzigjährigen Ehe hinterließ.

Die Informationen sind relativ spärlich, oft anekdotisch, und meist ohne Bezug zu seiner Arbeit. Er selbst veröffentlichte nur wenige Artikel.

Wir wissen jedoch, daß Pierre Paul Constant Chareau als Sohn von Ester Carvallo und Adolphe Chareau am 3. August 1883 in Bordeaux geboren wurde. Sein Vater war ursprünglich Weinhändler, zog aber, nachdem er sein Vermögen verloren hatte, nach Paris, wo er bei der Eisenbahn arbeitete. Pierre Chareau hatte eine Schwester. Ihrer eigenen Darstellung nach lernte Dollie (geborene Louise Dyte) ihren zukünftigen Ehemann kennen, als dieser sechzehn und sie selbst neunzehn Jahre alt war; sie heirateten fünf Jahre später, im Jahre 1904. Die Ehe blieb kinderlos. Die in England geborene und aufgewachsene Dollie verdiente zu Beginn ihrer Ehe ihr Geld mit Englischunterricht, während Pierre im Pariser Büro von Waring & Gillow arbeitete, einer großen englischen Firma, die auf Möbel und Innenarchitektur spezialisiert war. Er fing 1899 oder 1900 bei dieser Firma als technischer Zeichner an. Als er sie 1914 verließ, war er bereits erster Zeichner.

Unklar ist, welche Ausbildung Pierre Chareau nach dem Abschluß der höheren Schule genoß. Es gibt immer noch keinen Beweis dafür, daß Chareau als ordentlicher Student eine Architektenschule in Paris be-

en vigueur aux Beaux-Arts, il aurait toutefois facilement pu suivre des cours dans l'un des ateliers sans avoir à passer d'examen d'entrée pour s'inscrire officiellement; il aurait fort bien pu le faire le soir après son travail. Sous ce rapport, il est le type même de beaucoup de designers et architectes célèbres de son époque; comme Mies van der Rohe, Gerrit Rietveld, Frank Lloyd Wright et Le Corbusier, par exemple, Chareau a également dû apprendre son «métier» sur le tas plutôt que d'obtenir un diplôme avant de commencer sa carrière. Dans le cas de Chareau, cet «apprentissage» fut fait chez Waring & Gillow.

Cette firme britannique, qui avait des bureaux à Londres, Manchester, Liverpool, Glasgow et Paris, jouissait d'une clientèle internationale. Peu après 1900, elle publia un catalogue illustré fournissant des descriptions et des photographies de commandes exécutées par la compagnie. Il y avait là des banques, des bâtiments gouvernementaux, des clubs, des bureaux et des palais en Angleterre et à l'étranger (Afrique du sud, Japon, Siam, Amérique du nord et du sud), de même que des paquebots, des yachts royaux et des wagons. Waring & Gillow prétendaient qu'ils pouvaient fabriquer des intérieurs «d'époque», des imitations de meubles Chippendale et Sheraton, tout en soulignant qu'ils croyaient ardemment à la «modernité» et à un style honnête «dépouillé d'ornements».

A l'époque où Chareau travaillait dans les bureaux de Waring, la firme rénova de nombreux théâtres parisiens, dont la Gaîté, le Vaudeville, la Renaissance et l'Ambigu. Il y a tout lieu de supposer que Chareau participa à quelques-uns de ces projets – son œuvre ultérieure fut même considérablement influencée par ces derniers. Chareau nourrissait un amour profond pour la musique, la danse et les arts visuels; en 1905, sa femme écrivit au sujet de ses compositions musicales et de ses productions d'amateur, et raconte qu'ils allaient souvent plusieurs fois de suite au ballet et au théâtre.

Physiquement, Chareau était relativement petit, car il mesurait environ 1,60 m – une caractéristique ayant peut-être un rapport avec ses dessins de meubles ultérieurs qui semblent souvent bas pour des Européens moyens. Alors qu'il était frêle dans sa jeu-

work. In this regard, he is typical of many of the celebrated designers and architects of his day; like Mies van der Rohe, Gerrit Rietveld, Frank Lloyd Wright, and Le Corbusier, for example, Chareau too learned his *métier* on the job rather than obtaining a professional degree prior to beginning his career. In Chareau's case, this »apprenticeship« was served under Waring & Gillow.

The British firm, which had offices in London, Manchester, Liverpool and Glasgow as well as Paris, enjoyed a worldwide clientele. At some point after 1906 it published an illustrated catalogue providing descriptions and photographs of commissions which the company had executed. These ranged from banks, government buildings, clubs, offices and palaces in England and abroad (South Africa, Japan, Siam, North and South America) to steamships, royal yachts and railway cars. Waring & Gillow claimed they could produce »period« interiors, imitation Chippendale and Sheraton furniture, while insisting that they believed most ardently in »modernity« and an honest style »stripped of ornamentation«.

During the time that Chareau was working in the Waring offices, the firm renovated numerous Parisian theatres, including the Gaîté, Vaudeville, Renaissance, and Ambigu theatres. There is every reason to suppose that Chareau participated in some of these projects – indeed, his own later work was substantially influenced by them. Chareau nurtured a profound love of music and dance as well as of the visual arts; his wife writes of his musical compositions and amateur productions in 1905, and how they would often go to ballet and theatre productions many times over.

Physically, Chareau was relatively short in stature, measuring 5'2" (1.6 m) in height – a characteristic that may have some relevance to his later furniture designs, which often seem low in height to average Europeans. Slight of frame in his youth, he became more stout and balding in middle age, with his remaining hair worn long to the extent that one writer described him as having a »Louis XVI« appearance in 1930. Mobilised for military service during World War I, Chareau's independent professional career as a decorator began only with his discharge in 1919 at the age of thirty-five. His first client was to prove his most important and devoted in countless ways.

suchte. Er hätte jedoch in dem damaligen Studiensystem der Schönen Künste leicht Kurse in einem der Ateliers besuchen können, ohne die für die Anmeldung zum Studium erforderlichen Zulassungsprüfungen ablegen zu müssen; er hätte dies durchaus abends nach seiner Arbeit tun können.

Diese Art des Studiums war typisch für viele der gefeierten Designer und Architekten von damals. Ebenso wie z. B. Mies van der Rohe, Gerrit Rietveld, Frank Lloyd Wright und Le Corbusier hatte auch Chareau zu Beginn seiner Karriere keine akademische Ausbildung, sondern erlernte sein Metier eher in der Praxis. Seine »Lehrjahre« verbrachte er bei Waring & Gillow.

Die englische Firma, die Büros in London, Manchester, Liverpool und Glasgow und in Paris unterhielt, hatte Kunden in der ganzen Welt. Nach 1906 veröffentlichte sie einen Katalog mit Beschreibungen und Fotografien von Aufträgen, die die Firma ausgeführt hatte. Die Palette reichte von Banken, Regierungsgebäuden, Klubs, Büros und Palästen in England und im Ausland (Südafrika, Japan, Thailand, Nord- und Südamerika) bis hin zu Dampfschiffen, königlichen Jachten und Eisenbahnwagen. Waring & Gillow beteuerten zwar immer wieder, daß sie überaus leidenschaftliche Vertreter des »Modernen« und eines offenen Stils »frei von jeglicher Verzierung« seien, warben aber damit, »zeitgemäße« Inneneinrichtungen, nachgemachte Chippendale- und Sheratonmöbel herstellen zu können.

Während der Zeit, in der Chareau für die Waring-Büros arbeitete, renovierte die Firma zahlreiche Pariser Theater, unter anderem das Gaîté, das Vaudeville sowie das Renaissance und das Ambigu Theater. Chareau war an einigen dieser Projekte beteiligt, die unbestreitbar einen starken Einfluß auf seine späteren Arbeiten hatten.

Physisch war Chareau von kleiner Statur, er war nur 1,60 m groß – ein charakteristisches Merkmal, dem vielleicht eine gewisse Bedeutung für seine späteren Möbelentwürfe zukommt, da seine Möbel dem Durchschnittseuropäer oftmals sehr niedrig erscheinen. War er in seiner Jugend eher von schmächtiger Gestalt, so wurde er doch im mittleren Alter beleibter und verlor sein Kopfhaar. Dabei trug er das ihm verbliebene Haar so lang, daß ein Schreiber ihn im Jahre 1930 aufgrund seines Aussehens als »Louis XVI« bezeichnete.

nesse, il prit de l'embonpoint et devint chauve vers la cinquantaine; les cheveux qui lui restaient étaient si longs qu'en 1930, un écrivain dit de lui qu'il avait un air «Louis XVI».

Comme Chareau fut mobilisé pour le service militaire pendant la Première Guerre mondiale, sa carrière indépendante de décorateur commença seulement quand il fut rendu à la vie civile en 1919, à l'âge de 35 ans. Son premier client devait être le plus important et à tous égards le plus dévoué: c'était Annie Dalsace (née Bernheim), qui avait été à l'origine l'une des élèves de Dollie Chareau en 1905. Ses parents et elle étaient devenus par la suite des amis intimes des Chareau, et son nouveau mari, le docteur Jean Dalsace (repr. p. 10), se joignit au groupe en 1918. Ce fut pour l'appartement Dalsace situé au 195, boulevard Saint-Germain à Paris, que Chareau réalisa juste après la guerre les premiers meubles et les premiers intérieurs décorés que nous pouvons dater avec certitude. Pour Chareau comme pour bien d'autres de sa génération, les années de guerre marquèrent une rupture avec le passé. Sa longue phase de gestation et d'apprentissage, d'expérience pratique vitale, prit fin en 1914; elle fit place, à partir de 1919, à une nouvelle ère dans laquelle les Dalsace, leurs familles et amis lui fournirent des clients pour lesquels il put exercer ses talents.

Le premier contact de Chareau avec l'avant-garde artistique et un milieu bourgeois qui devait radicalement influencer son développement personnel était sans aucun doute davantage dû à la chance qu'à la richesse, au milieu social ou à une stratégie professionnelle. Nous n'avons pas d'informations concernant les amis de Chareau ou les collègues avec lesquels il travailla chez Waring avant la guerre ou bien encore les voyages qu'il effectua hors de France, sauf en Espagne. Il y a par conséquent tout lieu de croire que son premier contact avec les artistes avant-gardistes parisiens des années vingt était dû, une fois encore, aux Dalsace. Il rencontra par exemple Jean Lurçat, le peintre cubiste et dessinateur de tapisseries, grâce à Jean Dalsace qui était un ami intime de Lurçat depuis leur scolarité à Epinal. Lurçat, le frère de l'architecte André Lurçat, ne tarda pas à dessiner des tissus pour de nombreux meubles de Chareau (repr. p. 67). Le

This was Annie Dalsace (née Bernheim), who had originally been one of Dollie Chareau's pupils back in 1905. Both she and her parents had subsequently become close friends with the Chareaus, and in 1918 her new husband, the doctor Jean Dalsace (ill. p. 10), joined the circle. It was for the Dalsace apartment at 195 boulevard St. Germain in Paris during this immediate post-war period that Chareau executed the first pieces of furniture and the first decorated interiors that we can date with any certainty. For Chareau as for many others of his generation, the war years marked a break with the past. His lengthy phase of gestation and apprenticeship, of vital practical experience, ended in 1914; it gave way, as from 1919, to a new era in which the Dalsaces, their families and friends provided him with a circle of clients for whom he could exercise his talents.

Chareau's introduction in Paris both to the artistic avant-garde and to a bourgeois milieu which would radically influence his personal development undoubtedly owed more to chance than to wealth, social background or career strategy. We have no information about Chareau's circle of friends, nor about the colleagues with whom he worked at Waring's before the war, nor even about his travels outside of France, except to Spain. There is thus substantial reason to believe that his introduction to the Parisian avant-garde artists of the 1920s was again due to the Dalsaces. Jean Lurçat, for example, the Cubist painter and tapestry designer, he met through Jean Dalsace, who was a close friend of Lurçat from their schoolboy days in Epinal. Lurçat, the brother of architect André Lurçat, was soon designing the upholstery for many of Chareau's furniture pieces (ill. p. 67). The first of these was exhibited at the Paris Salon d'Automne in 1919. This and other personal introductions within a close-knit circle of friends, often leading to collaboration on a creative level, played a significant role in Chareau's career – particularly as he was not someone inclined to be self-promoting and publicity-seeking.

From the 1919 Salon onwards, the regular inclusion of his designs in public exhibitions not only led to other opportunities to exhibit (e.g. in the Salon des Artistes-Décorateurs as from 1922), but also brought

Chareaus berufliche Laufbahn als selbständiger Innenarchitekt begann erst bei seiner Entlassung aus dem Militärdienst im Jahre 1919, im Alter von fünfunddreißig Jahren. Sein erster Kunde erwies sich in vielerlei Hinsicht zugleich auch als sein wichtigster und treuester Kunde. Es war Annie Dalsace (geborene Bernheim), die ursprünglich im Jahre 1905 eine von Dollie Chareaus Schülerinnen gewesen war. Sie und ihre Eltern wurden später enge Freunde der Chareaus, und im Jahre 1918 gesellte sich auch ihr neuer Ehemann, der Arzt Jean Dalsace (Abb. S. 10), zu diesem Kreis. Die ersten Möbelstücke und Inneneinrichtungen, die wir mit einiger Sicherheit datieren können, entwarf Chareau während der Nachkriegsjahre für die Dalsacesche Wohnung am Boulevard St. Germain Nr. 195 in Paris. Für Chareau und für viele andere seiner Generation stellten die Kriegsjahre einen Bruch mit der Vergangenheit dar. Die überaus lange Phase seiner eigenen Entwicklung und Lehrzeit, und seiner grundlegenden praktischen Erfahrung, endete im Jahre 1914; sie wich von 1919 an einer neuen Ära, in der die Dalsaces, ihre Familie und ihre Freunde ihm zu einem Kundenkreis verhalfen, in dem er seine Talente entfalten konnte.

Chareaus Einführung in die Pariser Künstler-Avantgarde und das gehobene Bürgertum hatte nichts mit Reichtum, sozialer Herkunft oder gar Karrierestrategie zu tun, sondern war eher zufällig. Wir wissen nichts über Chareaus Freundeskreis, seine Kollegen, mit denen er vor dem Krieg bei Waring zusammenarbeitete, über seine Aufenthalte außerhalb Frankreichs, mit Ausnahme einer Spanienreise. Es besteht also Grund zu der Annahme, daß seine Einführung in die Pariser Künstler-Avantgarde der zwanziger Jahre ebenfalls den Dalsaces zuzuschreiben ist. So lernte er z. B. den kubistischen Maler und Designer von Dekorationsstoffen Jean Lurçat durch Jean Dalsace kennen; die beiden waren seit ihrer Schulzeit in Epinal eng befreundet. Lurçat, der Bruder des Architekten André Lurçat, entwarf schon bald die Polsterung für viele von Chareaus Möbelstücken (Abb. S. 67). Das erste dieser Stücke wurde bereits 1919 in der Pariser Ausstellung Salon d'Automne ausgestellt. Diese und andere Einführungen seiner Person in einen fest zusammengewachsenen Freundeskreis, die oftmals zu einer Zusammenarbeit auf

Pierre Chareau, vers 1930.
Pierre Chareau, c. 1930.
Pierre Chareau, um 1930.

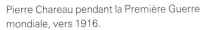

Pierre Chareau pendant la Première Guerre
mondiale, vers 1916.

Pierre Chareau during the First World War, c.
1916.

Pierre Chareau während des Ersten Weltkrie-
ges, um 1916.

Le docteur et Madame Dalsace dans la Maison
de Verre, 1955.

Doctor and Madame Dalsace in the Maison de
Verre, 1955.

Doktor und Madame Dalsace in der Maison de
Verre, 1955.

Conteneurs transformables en meubles, conçus par Chareau pour le gouvernement français, vers 1939.

Packing containers which turned into furniture, designed by Chareau for the French government, c. 1939.

Packcontainer, die in Möbelstücke verwandelt werden können, von Chareau für die französische Regierung entworfen, um 1939.

Premier Congrès International d'Architecture Moderne, 1928. Photo de groupe devant la chapelle du château La Sarraz.
De gauche à droite, debout: Mart Stam, Pierre Chareau, Victor Bourgeois, Max Haefeli, Pierre Jeanneret, Gerrit Rietveld, Rudolf Steiger, Ernst May, Alberto Sartoris, Gabriel Guevrékian, Hans Schmidt, Hugo Häring, Zavala, Florentin, Le Corbusier, Paul Artaria, Hélène de Mandrot, Friedrich Gubler, Rochat, André Lurçat, Robert von der Mühll, Maggioni, Huib Hoste, Sigfried Giedion, Werner Moser, Josef Frank.
De gauche à droite, assis: Garcia Mercadal, Molly Weber, Tadevossian.

First CIAM congress, 1928. Group photo in front of the Chapel of Castle La Sarraz.
From l., standing: Mart Stam, Pierre Chareau, Victor Bourgeois, Max Haefeli, Pierre Jeanneret, Gerrit Rietveld, Rudolf Steiger, Ernst May, Alberto Sartoris, Gabriel Guevrékian, Hans Schmidt, Hugo Häring, Zavala, Florentin, Le Corbusier, Paul Artaria, Hélène de Mandrot, Friedrich Gubler, Rochat, André Lurçat, Robert von der Mühll, Maggioni, Huib Hoste, Sigfried Giedion, Werner Moser, Josef Frank.
From l., seated: Garcia Mercadal, Molly Weber, Tadevossian.

Der erste CIAM-Kongreß, 1928. Gruppenfoto vor der Kapelle des Schlosses La Sarraz.
V. l. n. r. stehend: Mart Stam, Pierre Chareau, Victor Bourgeois, Max Haefeli, Pierre Jeanneret, Gerrit Rietveld, Rudolf Steiger, Ernst May, Alberto Sartoris, Gabriel Guevrékian, Hans Schmidt, Hugo Häring, Zavala, Florentin, Le Corbusier, Paul Artaria, Hélène de Mandrot, Friedrich Gubler, Rochat, André Lurçat, Robert von der Mühll, Maggioni, Huib Hoste, Sigfried Giedion, Werner Moser, Josef Frank.
V. l. n. r. sitzend: Garcia Mercadal, Molly Weber, Tadevossian.

premier fut exposé au Salon d'Automne à Paris en 1919. Ce premier contact et d'autres contacts personnels dans un cercle d'amis très uni, aboutissant souvent à une collaboration créatrice, joua un rôle important dans la carrière de Chareau – notamment parce qu'il n'était pas enclin à se faire de la publicité lui-même.

A partir du Salon de 1919, l'introduction régulière de ses dessins dans des expositions publiques amena non seulement d'autres occasions d'exposer (par exemple au Salon des Artistes Décorateurs à partir de 1922), mais le mit aussi en contact avec les leaders de l'avant-garde. Il forma de ce fait des associations durables avec les sculpteurs Jacques Lipchitz et Chana Orloff, le peintre Raoul Dufy, l'artiste décorateur Francis Jourdain (le fils de Frantz Jourdain) et Robert Mallet-Stevens, de même qu'avec des figures littéraires telles que Max Jacob (l'un de ses voisins, rue Nollet). Comme il devint membre des diverses organisations qui parrainaient ces expositions, Chareau fut non seulement en mesure de montrer des exemples de ses récents travaux, mais aussi invité à l'occasion à faire partie du jury qui sélectionnait les œuvres devant être exposées (renonçant ainsi à sa propre condition d'exposant). Dans l'intervalle, ses premières œuvres recevaient dans la presse des critiques favorables comme celle de Guillaume Janneau dans «Art et Décoration» en 1920. Les diverses expositions dans des salons et des galeries d'art étaient le meilleur moyen d'atteindre le public le plus vaste possible. Contrairement à d'autres designers établis de l'époque, tels que Maurice Dufrêne et Paul Follot, Chareau ne fut jamais lié commercialement à l'un des grands ateliers attachés aux grands magasins, comme «La Maîtrise» aux Galeries Lafayette ou «La Pomone» au Bon Marché.

Ses façons non commerciales peuvent être partiellement attribuées à certains traits de sa personnalité, qui peuvent à leur tour expliquer pourquoi son atelier et son magasin étaient relativement modestes. Chareau était un perfectionniste pour tout ce qui concernait sa propre production. Nathalie Dombre, dont le mari, André de Heering, commença à travailler avec Chareau en 1937, raconte dans une interview accordée à Marc Vellay (1984) qu'il refaisait ses plans plusieurs fois, à grands frais, avant

him into contact with leaders of the avant-garde. He thereby forged lasting associations with sculptors Jacques Lipchitz and Chana Orloff, painter Raoul Dufy, artist-decorator Francis Jourdain (the son of Frantz Jourdain) and Robert Mallet-Stevens, as well as with literary figures such as Max Jacob (a neighbour of his in the rue Nollet). As he became a member of the various organizations which sponsored these exhibitions, Chareau was not only able to show examples of his recent work, but was also invited on occasions to serve on the jury which selected the works to be shown (thereby relinquishing his own position as an exhibitor). Meanwhile, his early work was remarked upon favourably in the press by critics such as Guillaume Janneau in »Art et Décoration« in 1920. The various salons and gallery exhibitions represented the most important means by which his work reached the widest possible public. Unlike other established designers of the time, such as Maurice Dufrêne and Paul Follot, Chareau never became commercially linked to any of the large ateliers attached to department stores such as »La Maîtrise« at Galeries Lafayette or »La Pomone« at au Bon Marché.

This non-commercial approach may be attributable in part to certain traits in his personality, which may in turn explain why he maintained a relatively modest atelier and shop. Chareau was a perfectionist as far as his own production was concerned. Nathalie Dombre, whose husband, André de Heering, began working with Chareau in 1937, recounts in an interview with Marc Vellay (1984) how he would have the plans for a project redone many times over, and at considerable expense, before he was satisfied. Bearing in mind that Chareau was also reputed to be hypersensitive, depressive on occasion, stubborn and difficult in his relations with others, it is not surprising that he preferred to work within a relatively closed network of clients and craftsmen where mutual confidence prevailed.

His manner of working with clients and close collaborators is revealing, and at the same time somewhat contradictory in terms of his perfectionism. Pierre Vago, the first editor of »L'Architecture d'Aujourd'hui« in the 1930s, accompanied Chareau on one occasion to an appointment with his cabinet-maker (»ébeniste«) at an apart-

kreativer Ebene führten, spielte neben anderem eine entscheidende Rolle in Chareaus Laufbahn – besonders deshalb, weil er nicht dazu neigte, sich selbst zu avancieren und Publicity zu suchen.

Seit der Ausstellung im Jahre 1919 wurden seine Entwürfe regelmäßig in öffentliche Ausstellungen einbezogen. Dies führte nicht nur zu weiteren Ausstellungsmöglichkeiten (wie z. B. im Salon des Artistes-Décorateurs, von 1922 an), sondern brachte ihm auch den Kontakt zu den Führern der Avantgarde. Dabei schuf er dauerhafte Verbindungen nicht nur zu den Bildhauern Jacques Lipchitz und Chana Orloff, dem Maler Raoul Dufy, dem Kunstdekorateur Francis Jourdain (dem Sohn von Frantz Jourdain) und Robert Mallet-Stevens, sondern auch zu literarischen Persönlichkeiten wie Max Jacob (einer seiner Nachbarn in der Rue Nollet). Durch seine Mitgliedschaft in einer der vielen Organisationen, die Ausstellungen sponserten, war er nicht nur in der Lage, einige Beispiele seiner neuesten Arbeiten zu zeigen, sondern wurde gelegentlich auch aufgefordert, der Jury beizutreten, die die auszustellenden Werke auswählte (dadurch verzichtete er dann darauf, selbst auszustellen). Mittlerweile äußerten sich Kritiker, wie z. B. Guillaume Janneau in »Art et Décoration« im Jahre 1920, in der Presse positiv über sein frühes Werk. Die vielen Ausstellungen in den Salons und Galerien stellten das wichtigste Mittel dar, um seine Werke einer möglichst breiten Öffentlichkeit zugänglich zu machen. Anders als andere etablierte Designer seiner Zeit, wie beispielsweise Maurice Dufrêne oder Paul Follot, hatte Chareau nie geschäftlich mit einem der großen Ateliers zu tun, die an Fachgeschäfte wie z. B. »La Maîtrise« an den Galeries Lafayette oder »La Pomone« am Au Bon Marché angegliedert waren.

Diese unkommerzielle Einstellung kann teilweise bestimmten Charakterzügen Chareaus zugeschrieben werden, was erklärt, warum er nur ein relativ bescheidenes Atelier und Geschäft unterhielt. Was seine eigene Produktion anbelangte, war Chareau ein Perfektionist. Nathalie Dombre, deren Ehemann André de Heering im Jahre 1937 begann, mit Chareau zusammenzuarbeiten, berichtet in einem Interview mit Marc Vellay (1984), wie er die Pläne für ein Projekt viele Male erneuert haben wollte, bevor er mit ihnen zufrieden

d'être satisfait. Si l'on tient compte du fait que Chareau était également connu pour son hypersensibilité, ses dépressions occasionnelles, son obstination et son caractère difficile, on n'est pas surpris qu'il ait préféré travailler à l'intérieur d'un réseau relativement fermé de clients et d'artisans où la confiance mutuelle était de mise.

Sa façon de travailler avec ses clients et ses proches collaborateurs est révélatrice et en même temps quelque peu contradictoire eu égard à son perfectionnisme. Pierre Vago, le premier rédacteur en chef de «L'Architecture d'Aujourd'hui» dans les années trente, accompagna un jour Chareau à un rendez-vous avec l'ébéniste dans un appartement en cours de restauration; Chareau donna verbalement ses instructions pour l'exécution d'un nouveau meuble destiné à un endroit précis dans la pièce, y ajoutant seulement quelques gestes et une vague esquisse sur place. Chareau ne se fiait pas aux dessins précis et détaillés à l'avance, et il y a de bonnes raisons de croire qu'il n'était pas un dessinateur particulièrement doué. En fait, il préférait sans aucun doute travailler sur le chantier. En une autre circonstance – peut-être apocryphe – rapportée par Vago, Chareau reçut un coup de téléphone dingue d'une cliente affolée dont il venait de redécorer l'appartement et qui avait découvert, à la veille du dîner d'inauguration, que la salle à manger était trop sombre à cause de l'éclairage insuffisant et aussi du plafond qui avait été peint en noir. Chareau, qui avait demandé à son éclairagiste André Salomon de l'accompagner, partit précipitamment dans la nuit pour voir ce qui avait besoin d'être modififié – la couleur du plafond ou l'éclairage![2]

Chareau était un être passionné, véhément dans son appréciation de la qualité que ce soit chez les gens ou dans les choses. Il ne regardait pas à la dépense quand il s'agissait d'obtenir la meilleure qualité possible dans l'exécution de ses instructions. La profondeur de l'attachement et de la tendresse qu'il avait pour sa femme apparaît aussi, en termes à la fois affectifs et poétiques, dans les rares lettres qui nous sont parvenues, de même que son attachement envers ses fidèles amis et protecteurs, les Dalsace.

Sa collection d'œuvres contemporaines laisse également voir ses passions et ses goûts en matière d'art. Son appartement

ment under renovation; Chareau's directions for a new piece of furniture to be executed for a particular place in the room were communicated verbally, with just a few gestures and a vague sketch on the spot. Chareau did not rely on precise, detailed drawings in advance of any product, and there is reason to believe that he was not a particularly talented draughtsman. In fact, he undoubtedly preferred to work on the building site itself. On another – perhaps apocryphal – occasion, according to Vago, Chareau received a frantic call from a woman client whose apartment he had just redecorated and who had discovered, on the eve of the inaugural dinner, that the dining room was too gloomy because of insufficient lighting and/or the ceiling which had been painted black. Chareau, having called his lighting specialist André Salomon to join him, dashed off into the night to see what needed to be modified – the ceiling colour or the lighting![2]

Chareau was a passionate individual, intense in his appreciation of quality wherever he found it, both in people and things. He spared no expense when it came to achieving the highest possible quality in the execution of his commissions. The depth of his attachment to and tenderness for his wife also emerges, in terms both emotional and poetic, from the few surviving letters addressed to her, together with his devotion to his most loyal friends and benefactors, the Dalsaces.

Passionate conviction is revealed also in his tastes, especially in his collection of contemporary works of art. His apartment at 54 rue Nollet (ill. p. 76/77) housed a number of works by Paul Klee, Juan Gris, Braque, Picasso, Chagall, Max Ernst, Lipchitz and even Modigliani, whose famous caryatid Chareau acquired soon after the artist's death in 1920 on the advice of Lipchitz, and which stood in his rue Nollet garden for many years. Significant, too, is the fact that in 1928 Chareau bought the second painting sold by Mondrian in France (the first having been bought by the Vicomte de Noailles, one of Chareau's own patrons, in 1926).[3] Chareau would often hang works from his collection in exhibitions of his own furniture, not so much to promote the work itself as to demonstrate underlying affinities of poetic sensibility or vocabulary of form. One of the most il-

war. Wenn man bedenkt, daß Chareau außerdem in seiner Beziehung zu anderen Menschen als äußerst sensibel, gelegentlich depressiv, eigensinnig und schwierig galt, verwundert es nicht, daß er lieber innerhalb eines geschlossenen Netzes von Auftraggebern und Handwerkern arbeitete, in dem gegenseitiges Vertrauen herrschte.

Seine Art, mit Kunden und engen Mitarbeitern zu arbeiten, ist sehr aufschlußreich und steht zugleich ein wenig im Widerspruch zu seinem Perfektionismus. Pierre Vago, in den dreißiger Jahren der erste Herausgeber von »L'Architecture d'Aujourd'hui«, begleitete Chareau einmal zu einem Termin mit seinem Möbeltischler (»ébeniste«) in eine Wohnung, die gerade renoviert wurde; Chareau erteilte seine Anweisungen für ein neues Möbelstück, das für einen beonderen Platz im Raum angefertigt werden sollte, lediglich verbal, mit nur wenigen Gesten und einer vagen Skizze an der Stelle, wo das Möbel später stehen sollte. Er verließ sich nicht auf präzise, detaillierte Entwürfe, die dem Produkt vorausgingen, und es besteht Grund zu der Annahme, daß er nicht einmal ein besonders talentierter Zeichner war. Tatsächlich arbeitete er lieber auf der Baustelle selbst. Bei einer anderen Gelegenheit soll Chareau – Vago zufolge – einen verzweifelten Anruf einer Kundin erhalten haben, deren Wohnung er gerade erst neu dekoriert hatte. Die Kundin hatte, kurz bevor das Einweihungsessen stattfinden sollte, entdeckt, daß das Eßzimmer zu düster sei, entweder weil die Beleuchtung nicht ausreichte und/oder wegen der Decke, die schwarz gestrichen worden war. Chareau, der inzwischen seinen Beleuchtungsspezialisten André Salomon zu sich gerufen hatte, stürzte hinaus in die Nacht, um zu sehen, was geändert werden mußte – die Farbe der Decke oder die Beleuchtung![2]

Chareau war ein leidenschaftlicher Mensch, der Qualität besonders zu schätzen wußte, wo immer er auf sie stieß, sowohl bei Menschen als auch bei Gegenständen. Er scheute keine Kosten, wenn es galt, die bestmögliche Qualität bei der Ausführung seiner Aufträge zu erzielen. Die tiefe Zuneigung und Zärtlichkeit, die er für seine Frau empfand, geht in emotionalen und poetischen Worten aus den wenigen hinterbliebenen Briefen an sie ebenso hervor wie seine Verehrung für seine

au 54, rue Nollet (repr. p. 76/77), abritait nombre d'œuvres de Paul Klee, Juan Gris, Braque, Picasso, Chagall, Max Ernst et Lipchitz; Chareau fit même l'acquisition de la fameuse caryatide de Modigliani peu après la mort de l'artiste, en 1920, sur le conseil de Lipchitz, et elle resta dans son jardin de la rue Nollet pendant de nombreuses années. Le fait que Chareau ait acheté en 1928 la seconde peinture vendue en France par Mondrian (la première avait été achetée par le Vicomte de Noailles, l'un des clients de Chareau, en 1926), est également significatif. Chareau accrochait souvent des œuvres de sa collection dans des expositions de ses propres meubles, moins pour promouvoir l'œuvre elle-même que pour démontrer les affinités sous-jacentes de la sensibilité poétique ou du vocabulaire formel. L'un des meilleurs exemples de son attirance pour une certaine ligne «métaphysique» du surréalisme est le fait qu'il ait choisi une peinture de De Chirico pour une exposition de meubles à la galerie Barbazanges en 1926.

Afin de promouvoir – à regret, toutefois – son propre travail et celui de quelques amis artistes comme Hélène Henry, Jean Burkhalter et d'autres encore, Chareau ouvrit en 1924 un petit magasin dans la rue du Cherche-Midi. «La Boutique», comme l'appelait Chareau, était située juste à côté de la galerie d'art de Jeanne Bucher, l'une des premières adeptes enthousiastes de la peinture avant-gardiste à Paris et amie de Chareau et des Dalsace. Il y avait là – à côté de quelques pièces originales, sans doute – un catalogue de photographies illustrant des meubles qu'il avait créés et montrant des vues de stands d'exposition et d'intérieurs qu'il avait conçus. Les clients potentiels pouvaient étudier l'album de grand format qui contenait des reproductions en noir et blanc faites par des photographes professionnels tels que l'Américaine Thérèse Bonney.

En 1925, Chareau était un membre bien établi d'un cercle d'architectes-décorateurs, parfois appelés «ensembliers» (plutôt que simplement décorateurs), qui prirent part à l'Exposition Internationale des Arts Décoratifs et Industriels Modernes à Paris. Le fait que Chareau ait collaboré avec Mallet-Stevens, Guévrékian, Lurçat et Lipchitz à la conception d'une ambassade de France parrainée pour l'Exposition par la Société des Artistes Décorateurs montre

luminating examples of his attraction to a certain »metaphysical« line of Surrealism is his choice of a De Chirico painting for inclusion in an exhibition of furniture at the Barbazanges gallery in 1926.

In order to promote – however reluctantly – both his own work and that of a few artist friends such as Hélène Henry, Jean Burkhalter and others, in 1924 Chareau opened a tiny shop on the rue du Cherche-Midi. »La Boutique«, as Chareau's shop was called, was located next door to the art gallery run by Jeanne Bucher, an early and strong proponent of avant-garde painting in Paris and a friend of Chareau and the Dalsaces. Here – alongside, one supposes, a few original pieces – he kept a catalogue of photographs illustrating items of furniture of his own creation and showing views of exhibition stands and interiors which he had designed. Potential clients could study the album of large-format, black-and-white reproductions by professional photographers like the American Thérèse Bonney.

By 1925 Chareau was a well-established member of a circle of architect/decorators, sometimes referred to as »ensembliers« (rather than simply decorators), who took part in the Exposition Internationale des Arts Décoratifs et Industriels Modernes in Paris. Indicative of his sense of »team spirit«, which manifested itself on numerous occasions, Chareau collaborated with Mallet-Stevens, Guévrékian, Lurçat and Lipchitz on the conception of a French Embassy, sponsored for the Exposition by the Société des Artistes-Décorateurs. His furniture designs, which had already appeared in the atelier-house designed by Le Corbusier for Lipchitz in 1925, soon found their way into the homes of the Vicomte de Noailles and the couturier Jacques Heim. The 1925 Exposition was also the occasion of another important encounter; it was here that Chareau met the Dutch architect Bernard Bijvoët, who in 1926 was to become his assistant on his first major architectural commission, the Clubhouse at Beauvallon in southern France (ill. p. 92). It was Bijvoët, too, who collaborated with Chareau on the masterpiece to follow, the Maison de Verre for the Dalsaces.

It comes as no surprise, therefore, to find Chareau among the group of architects from France who met in the villa of Madame de Mandrot in La Sarraz, Switzer-

treuesten Freunde und Wohltäter, die Dalsaces.

Seine leidenschaftliche Überzeugung verrät sich auch in seinem Geschmack, besonders in seiner Sammlung zeitgenössischer Kunstwerke. Seine Wohnung in der Rue Nollet Nr. 54 (Abb. S. 76/77) beherbergte zahlreiche Werke von Paul Klee, Juan Gris, Braque, Picasso, Chagall, Max Ernst, Lipchitz und Modigliani, dessen berühmte »Karyatide« er auf Anraten von Lipchitz bald nach dem Tod des Künstlers im Juli 1920 erwarb und die viele Jahre in seinem Garten in der Rue Nollet stand. Bemerkenswert ist auch, daß Chareau das zweite Gemälde 1928 bei Mondrian in Frankreich erstand.[3] Bei den Ausstellungen seiner eigenen Möbel hängte Chareau oftmals Gemälde aus seiner Sammlung auf, nicht so sehr um für das Werk selbst zu werben, sondern um die grundlegenden Ähnlichkeiten des kreativen Empfindens oder das Vokabular der Form zu demonstrieren. Ein Beispiel dafür, wie sehr er sich zu einer gewissen »metaphysischen« Linie des Surrealismus hingezogen fühlte, ist das von ihm ausgewählte Gemälde von De Chirico, das er 1926 in eine Möbelausstellung in der Gallerie Barbazanges miteinbezog.

Um für seine eigenen Werke und die einiger befreundeter Künstler, wie beispielsweise Hélène Henry, Jean Burkhalter und andere, zu werben, eröffnete Chareau 1924 einen kleinen Laden an der Rue du Cherche Midi; »La Boutique« befand sich unmittelbar neben einer Kunstgalerie, die von Jeanne Bucher geleitet wurde, einer frühen und energischen Verfechterin der avantgardistischen Malerei in Paris und Freundin von Chareau und den Dalsaces. Hier hatte er – vermutlich neben einigen Originalstücken – einen Katalog, mit Fotografien von Möbelstücken, die er selbst entworfen hatte, zusammengestellt. Außerdem enthielt der Katalog Ansichten von Ausstellungsstandorten seiner Möbel und von ihm entworfene Innendekorationen. Potentielle Kunden konnten das Album im Großformat mit Schwarzweißfotos von professionellen Fotografen, wie z. B. der Amerikanerin Thérèse Bonney, eingehend studieren.

Im Jahre 1925 war Chareau festes Mitglied eines gelegentlich als »ensembliers« (mehr als nur Innenarchitekten) bezeichneten Architekten- und Dekorateurkreises,

qu'il avait l'«esprit d'équipe», qui se manifesta en diverses occasions. Ses meubles, qui avaient déjà paru dans la maison-atelier dessinée par Le Corbusier pour Lipchitz en 1925, firent bientôt leur chemin dans les demeures du Vicomte de Noailles et du couturier Jacques Heim. L'exposition de 1925 fut également l'occasion d'une autre rencontre importante; c'est en effet là que Chareau rencontra l'architecte hollandais Bernard Bijvoët qui devint son assistant en 1926 pour sa première grande commande architecturale, le club de Beauvallon dans le sud de la France (repr. p. 92). Ce fut également Bijvoët qui collabora avec Chareau au chef d'œuvre suivant, la Maison de Verre pour les Dalsace.

Il n'est donc pas surprenant de trouver Chareau parmi le groupe d'architectes français qui se retrouvèrent en juin 1928 dans la villa de Madame de Mandrot à La Sarraz, en Suisse, pour fonder le Congrès International d'Architecture Moderne (CIAM) (repr. p. 11). Outre le club de Beauvallon, Chareau avait également été chargé de rénover le Grand Hôtel de Tours (repr. p. 87/88) pour Paul Bernheim (un cousin d'Annie Dalsace), et dessinait en outre les premiers plans pour la Maison de Verre; son autorité artistique et morale était donc déjà acceptée parmi ces architectes du mouvement moderne. Quand un groupe de designers et d'architectes se sépara de la Société des Artistes Décorateurs en 1929 pour former l'Union des Artistes Modernes (UAM), Chareau se trouvait parmi les fondateurs, avec Francis Jourdain, Mallet-Stevens et d'autres encore.

En 1931, Chareau eut beaucoup de publicité, surtout dans la presse populaire, pour ce qui concerne la Maison de Verre des Dalsace qui était presque achevée. A cette époque, il travailla également à plusieurs intérieurs pour les familles Dreyfus (repr. p. 96/97) et Fahri (repr. p. 94/95), de même que pour les bureaux de LTT (repr. p. 100), une compagnie de télégraphe et téléphone parisienne. Dans l'intervalle, une nouvelle revue – «L'Architecture d'Aujourd'hui» –, dont les tendances idéologiques devaient être étroitement associées au mouvement moderne en architecture, fut fondée. André Bloc invita Chareau à devenir membre de son conseil de rédaction. Il fut membre actif du conseil et fit partie du jury des concours que la revue organisa pendant les années trente.

land, in June 1928 to found the Congrès Internationale d'Architecture Moderne (CIAM) (ill. p. 11). In addition to the Clubhouse at Beauvallon, Chareau had also been commissioned to renovate the Grand Hotel in Tours (ill. p. 87/88) for Paul Bernheim (a cousin of Annie Dalsace), and was furthermore drawing up the first plans for the Maison de Verre; his artistic and moral authority among these architects of the Modern Movement was thus already accepted. When a group of designers and architects broke away from the Société des Artistes-Décorateurs in 1929 to form the Union des Artistes Modernes (UAM), Chareau was amongst the founders, together with Francis Jourdain, Mallet-Stevens and others.

In 1931 Chareau received much publicity, particularly in the popular press, with regard to the Dalsaces' Maison de Verre, which was nearing completion. He was also working on several interiors at the time, for the Dreyfus (ill. p. 96/97) and Fahri (ill. p. 94/95) families and for the offices of LTT (ill. p. 100), a telephone and telegraph company in Paris. Meanwhile, a new magazine was being put together – »L'Architecture d'Aujourd'hui« – whose ideological tendencies were to be closely associated with the Modern Movement in architecture. Chareau was invited by André Bloc to be a member of its editorial advisory board. He was an active member of the board and sat on the jury of the competitions which the magazine organized throughout the 1930s.

Although Chareau's age, experience and artistic stature should perhaps have made him better placed than many others to obtain work – especially as a furniture designer – in the mid–1930s, the number of his commissions nevertheless declined. He participated in a limited way in the Paris Exposition of 1937; the same year, he designed the small weekend house west of Paris for the dancer Djémil Anik (ill. p. 101). By the close of the decade and the dawn of World War II in 1939, Chareau was working on a design project for the French government, namely packing containers which the colonial military forces could transform into essential pieces of furnishing once they had arrived at their destination (ill. p. 11).

Shortly after German forces invaded France, Chareau left the country via Spain

dessen Mitglieder an der Exposition Internationale des Arts Décoratifs et Industriels Modernes in Paris teilnahmen. Sein Sinn für »Teamgeist«, den er bei zahlreichen Gelegenheiten bewies, zeigt sich auch in der Zusammenarbeit mit Mallet-Stevens, Guévrékian, Lurçat und Lipchitz bei dem Entwurf für die französische Botschaft, der für die Exposition von der Société des Artistes-Décorateurs gesponsert wurde. Seine Möbelentwürfe, die bereits in dem Atelierhaus ausgestellt worden waren, das Le Corbusier für Lipchitz im Jahre 1925 entworfen hatte, fanden schon bald ihren Weg in die Wohnungen des Vicomte de Noailles und des Couturiers Jacques Heim. Die Exposition im Jahre 1925 führte Chareau mit dem niederländischen Architekten Bernard Bijvoët zusammen, der 1926 sein Assistent bei seinem ersten größeren Bauauftrag, dem Klubhaus in Beauvallon in Südfrankreich (Abb. S. 92), werden sollte. Bijvoët war es dann auch, der mit Chareau an dessen nachfolgendem Meisterwerk, der Maison de Verre für die Dalsaces, zusammenarbeitete.

Es ist deshalb nicht weiter verwunderlich, Chareau in einer Gruppe von Architekten aus Frankreich zu finden, die im Juni 1928 in der Villa von Madame de Mandrot in La Sarraz, in der Schweiz, zusammenkamen, um den Congrès Internationale d'Architecture Moderne (CIAM; Abb. S. 11) zu gründen. Zusätzlich zu dem Klubhaus in Beauvallon wurde Chareau auch damit beauftragt, das Grand Hotel in Tours (Abb. S. 87/88) für Paul Bernheim (ein Cousin von Annie Dalsace) zu renovieren, und war überdies damit beschäftigt, die ersten Entwürfe für die Maison de Verre zu fertigen; seine künstlerische und moralische Autorität unter diesen Architekten der Modernen Bewegung wurde also bereits akzeptiert. Als sich im Jahre 1929 eine Gruppe von Architekten und Designern von der Société des Artistes-Décorateurs trennte, um die Union des Artistes Modernes (UAM) zu gründen, befand sich Chareau zusammen mit Francis Jourdain, Mallet-Stevens und anderen unter den Gründungsmitgliedern. 1931 erregte er, besonders in der Tagespresse, wegen der Dalsaceschen Maison de Verre, die sich ihrer Vollendung näherte, einiges Aufsehen. Gleichzeitig arbeitete er noch an Inneneinrichtungen für die Familien Dreyfus (Abb. S. 96/97) und Fahri (Abb. S. 94/95) und die Büros von LTT (Abb.

15

Bien que l'âge, l'expérience et l'importance artistique de Chareau l'eussent peut-être mieux placé que beaucoup d'autres pour obtenir du travail – spécialement comme designer – au milieu des années trente, le nombre de commandes diminua malgré tout. Il participa de manière restreinte à l'Exposition parisienne de 1937; la même année, il dessina pour la danseuse Djémil Anik une petite maison de week-end à l'ouest de Paris (repr. p. 101). A la fin de la décennie et à l'aube de la Seconde Guerre mondiale en 1939, Chareau travailla à un projet pour le gouvernement français, à savoir des conteneurs que les forces militaires coloniales pouvaient transformer en meubles indispensables une fois parvenus à destination (repr. p. 11).

Peu après que les armées allemandes eurent envahi la France, Chareau quitta le pays pour le Maroc via l'Espagne. Là, il obtint un visa pour les Etats-Unis où il arriva en octobre 1940 – suivi de sa femme Dollie un an plus tard. Il vécut à New York où il travailla pour l'attaché culturel français et organisa des expositions. Beaucoup de ses vieux amis parisiens, dont Lipchitz et Max Ernst, le rejoignirent pendant la guerre.

Comme il n'était pas certain des perspectives d'avenir qui lui étaient ouvertes en France après 1945, il décida de rester à New York. L'unique grand projet architectural qu'il réalisa pendant cette période fut une maison de week-end à Long Island pour le jeune peintre Robert Motherwell (repr. p. 101). C'était, plus précisément, un «aménagement» de hutte préfabriquée qu'il transforma et meubla pour Motherwell. Chareau mourut à New York en 1950 sans être retourné en France.

to Morocco. Here he obtained a visa for the United States, arriving there in October 1940 – to be followed by his wife Dollie a year later. Living in New York City, he worked for the French Cultural Attaché organizing exhibitions. A number of his old friends from Paris joined him during the war years, including Lipchitz and Max Ernst.

Uncertain about the career opportunities left open to him in France after 1945, he decided to remain in New York. His only significant architectural project during this period was a weekend house on Long Island for the young painter Robert Motherwell (ill. p. 101). It was, more accurately, a »conversion« of a Quonset hut which he transformed and furnished for Motherwell. Chareau died in New York in 1950 without having returned to France.

S. 100), einer Telefon- und Telegraphengesellschaft in Paris. Unterdessen wurde ein neues Magazin zusammengestellt – »L'Architecture d'Aujourd'hui« –, dessen ideologische Tendenzen eng mit der Modernen Architekturbewegung verbunden werden sollten. Auf André Blocs Wunsch hin wurde Chareau Mitglied des redaktionellen Beratungsausschusses und saß in der Jury, die die Gewinner der Wettbewerbe ermittelte, die das Magazin während der dreißiger Jahre veranstaltete.

Man sollte annehmen, daß Chareau – besonders als Möbeldesigner – aufgrund seines Alters, seiner Erfahrung und seines künstlerischen Rangs Mitte der dreißiger Jahre eher Aufträge erhielt als andere seiner Kollegen, doch ging die Zahl seiner Aufträge zurück. An der Pariser Ausstellung von 1937 nahm er nur in kleinem Umfang teil; im selben Jahr entwarf er für die Tänzerin Djémil Anik im Westen von Paris ein kleines Wochenendhaus (Abb. S. 101). Zu Beginn des Zweiten Weltkriegs im Jahre 1939 arbeitete Chareau an einem Designprojekt für die französische Regierung. Es handelte sich hierbei um den Entwurf von Verpackungscontainern, die die Kolonialsoldaten in Möbelstücke umwandeln konnten, sobald sie an ihrem Bestimmungsort angelangt waren (Abb. S. 11).

Kurz nachdem die deutschen Truppen in Frankreich einmarschiert waren, verließ Chareau sein Land und reiste über Spanien nach Marokko. Hier erhielt er dann ein Visum für die Vereinigten Staaten von Amerika, wo er im Oktober 1940 eintraf. Seine Frau Dollie folgte ihm ein Jahr später. Er lebte in New York City und arbeitete für den französischen Kulturattaché, indem er Ausstellungen organisierte. Während der Kriegsjahre stießen viele seiner alten Freunde aus Paris zu ihm, darunter auch Lipchitz und Max Ernst.

Da seine Karriere in Frankreich nach 1945 nur sehr ungewiß war, entschloß er sich, in New York zu bleiben. Sein einziges bedeutendes Bauprojekt während dieser Zeit war das Wochenendhaus für den jungen Maler Robert Motherwell auf Long Island (Abb. S. 101). Genauer gesagt, handelte es sich hierbei um den »Umbau« einer Nissenhütte, die er für Motherwell umänderte und möblierte. Chareau starb im Jahre 1950 in New York, ohne Frankreich noch einmal wiedergesehen zu haben.

Son œuvre

L'œuvre de Pierre Chareau résiste à l'interprétation conventionnelle au sein du mouvement moderne dans la France des années vingt et trente. Ceci est dû à la forme de la maison-familiale-avec-cabinet-médical des Dalsace, connue sous le nom de Maison de Verre, la principale œuvre de Chareau dont la construction dura environ quatre ans. Alors que les plans antérieurs de Chareau et son étroite collaboration avec le maître ferronnier Dalbet permettent de mieux comprendre la phase préliminaire qui aboutit à la commande Dalsace, la Maison de Verre elle-même marque une rupture dans les conceptions de l'artiste et dans sa façon d'aborder le design moderne. Malgré tout, la production de Chareau n'arriva pas à la hauteur des qualités classiques intrinsèques et de la signification potentiellement révolutionnaire de la Maison de Verre dans les années qui suivirent.

Mais c'est là que se trouve le paradoxe – comment une œuvre d'art ou d'architecture peut-elle être à la fois «classique» et «révolutionnaire»? Peut-elle être perçue et interprétée de telle ou telle façon à l'époque de sa création, puis de manière différente trente, quarante ou même cent ans après? Quand on regarde les dessins novateurs (mais toujours indéniablement bourgeois) de meubles et d'intérieurs exécutés par Chareau avant 1928 et qu'on les compare aux œuvres importantes de ses contemporains, on est frappé par l'énorme gouffre qui les sépare de la Maison de Verre en tant que «Gesamtkunstwerk» ou «œuvre d'art totale». Tandis que des meubles particuliers peuvent présenter des caractéristiques «classiques» – dans les qualités universelles et éternellement satisfaisantes de leurs proportions ou formes, par exemple –, il faut bien davantage pour qualifier de «classique» une maison ou un bâtiment. Elle doit en effet capter l'essence d'une culture universelle, de ce qu'Adolf Loos appelait «cet équilibre de l'homme intérieur et de l'homme extérieur qui est la condition de toute pensée et de toute activité raisonnable».[4] Le véritable test de l'importance classique de la Maison de Verre de Chareau, de son caractère rationnel et éternel est que les visiteurs étrangers, de cultures non-occidentales aussi bien japo-

His Work

The œuvre of Pierre Chareau resists conventional interpretation within the Modern Movement in France of the 1920s and 1930s. The reason for this difficulty is found in the shape of the Dalsace family-home-cum-medical-practice known as the Maison de Verre, the major work of Chareau's career which took some four years to complete. While Chareau's previous design work, and his close collaboration with Dalbet the master metalworker, offer fundamental insights into the preparatory phase which led up to the Dalsace commission, the Maison de Verre itself marks a rupture in the architect's conceptions and approach to modern design. Yet Chareau's production in subsequent years failed to match the intrinsic classical qualities and potentially revolutionary import of the Maison de Verre.

But here lies a paradox – for how can a work of art or architecture be both »classical« and »revolutionary«? Can it be perceived and interpreted as one or the other at the time of its creation, and then differently thirty, forty or even one hundred years later? When we look at the innovative (but still undeniably bourgeois) furniture and interior designs by Chareau before 1928, and compare these with the significant work of his contemporaries, we are struck by the tremendous gulf that separates them from the Maison de Verre as a »Gesamtkunstwerk«, or »total work of art«. While individual pieces of furniture may reveal »classical« features – in the universal and eternally satisfying qualities of their proportions, shape or form, for example – for a house or a building to qualify as »classical« involves a great deal more. It must capture the essence of a universal culture, of what Adolf Loos termed »that equilibrium between the man's interior and exterior self which is the condition of all reasonable thought and activity«.[4] The true gauge of the classical stature of Chareau's glass house, of its rationality and its timelessness, is that visitors from all the world's cultures inevitably find some aspect with which to identify.

The Dalsace Maison de Verre has inspired an abundance of metaphors, which provide an essential indicator not only of the classical, archetypal nature of the house,

Seine Arbeit

Das Lebenswerk von Pierre Chareau läßt sich nicht mit der herkömmlichen Interpretation der Modernen Bewegung in Frankreich während der zwanziger und dreißiger Jahre in Einklang bringen. Der Grund für diese Schwierigkeit liegt in dem Dalsaceschen Familienhaus-mit-Arztpraxis, bekannt als Maison de Verre: dem Glanzstück seiner Karriere, zu dessen Vollendung er über vier Jahre brauchte. Während Chareaus vorangegangene Designarbeit und seine enge Zusammenarbeit mit dem führenden Metallverarbeiter Dalbet fundamentale Einblicke in die Vorbereitungsphase bieten, die schließlich zu dem Dalsace-Auftrag führte, bezeichnet die Maison de Verre selbst einen Bruch in den Entwürfen des Architekten und in seiner Annäherung an das moderne Design. Dennoch läßt sich Chareaus späteres Werk nicht mit den eigentlich klassischen Eigenschaften und der möglicherweise revolutionären Bedeutung der Maison de Verre vergleichen.

Doch hierin liegt ein Widerspruch – denn wie kann ein Kunst- oder Bauwerk sowohl »klassisch« als auch »revolutionär« sein? Kann ein Werk als das eine oder das andere zur Zeit seiner Entstehung verstanden werden, und in dreißig oder vierzig Jahren wieder anders? Wenn wir Chareaus innovative (aber unbestreitbar noch bürgerliche) Möbelentwürfe und seine Innenarchitektur vor 1928 betrachten und diese mit dem bedeutenden Werk seiner Zeitgenossen vergleichen, beeindruckt uns die gewaltige Kluft, die zwischen ihnen und der Maison de Verre als »Gesamtkunstwerk« steht. Während einzelne Möbelstücke »klassische« Züge aufweisen können – in ihren universellen Proportionen, Gestalt oder Form beispielsweise –, bedeutete es bei einem Haus oder Gebäude sehr viel mehr, wenn es als »klassisch« bezeichnet wird. Es mußte das Wesen der gesamten Kultur für sich einnehmen, was Adolf Loos als »dieses Gleichgewicht zwischen dem inneren und äußeren Selbst des Menschen, das die Bedingung für alles vernünftige Denken und Handeln ist«, bezeichnete.[4] Chareaus Haus aus Glas ist insofern wirklich klassisch, rational und zeitlos, als Besucher aus allen Kulturen der Welt zwangsläufig irgendeinen Aspekt finden, mit dem sie sich identifizieren können.

nais que musulmans, y trouvent inévitablement un aspect auquel ils peuvent s'identifier.

La Maison de Verre des Dalsace a inspiré une multitude de métaphores qui fournissent un indicateur essentiel, non seulement de la nature archétype classique de la maison, mais aussi de ses qualités révolutionnaires. A l'époque où la maison fut achevée, certains commentateurs pensèrent que ses espaces évoquaient les maisons avec patio de l'Andalousie mauresque, d'autres y virent un théâtre, un igloo esquimau (à cause de la façade en dalles de verre), ou même un bateau. De nos jours, les meubles encastrés, les écrans et panneaux coulissants, et les caractéristiques spatiales qui permettent une intimité visuelle tout en maintenant le contact acoustique à l'intérieur de l'habitation, ont incité des visiteurs japonais à la considérer comme traditionnellement japonaise – et un architecte chinois à remarquer que c'était vraiment «la demeure communiste idéale parce qu'elle est en fin de compte tout à fait transparente». Relativement peu de visiteurs «non initiés» de la Maison de Verre la quittent en disant qu'elle est «belle» – bien qu'il leur arrive d'être surpris, séduits et intrigués (et même rebutés à l'occasion). Néanmoins, ils trouvent presque toujours au moins une caractéristique – que ce soit les armoires de la chambre à coucher ou l'ensemble baignoire-bibliothèque (repr. p. 146) – qui semble ingénieuse, pratique ou poétique, et souvent «en avance sur son temps».

La compétence de Pierre Chareau et sa maîtrise suprême de son métier de concepteur s'accrurent pendant les années où il travailla comme dessinateur pour Waring & Gillow à Paris. Au cours de son ascension vers le poste de maître dessinateur, il participa à divers types de projets, commandes architecturales y comprises. Il fit connaissance et travailla avec de nombreux ébénistes du célèbre quartier du meuble parisien, dans la rue du Faubourg Saint-Antoine; c'est en effet vers la firme de Printz qu'il revint finalement quand il s'installa à son compte. L'ouvrage de référence le plus détaillé en matière de types de meubles, matériaux, formes et styles et le plus courant en Angleterre au tournant de siècle est «Das Englische Haus» (La maison anglais), une étude en trois volumes composée par Hermann Muthesius

Placard à tiroirs encastré dans la Maison de Verre.

Built-in chest of drawers in the Maison de Verre.

Eingebauter Schubladenschrank in der Maison de Verre.

but also of its revolutionary qualities. At the time of the house's completion, its spaces were thought by some commentators to evoke the courtyard houses of Moorish Andalusia, by others a theatre, an Eskimo igloo (because of the glass brick façade), even a ship.

In our own day, the built-in furniture, the sliding screens and panels, and the spatial features that permit visual privacy while maintaining acoustical contact within the dwelling, lead Japanese visitors to see it as traditionally Japanese – and a Chinese architect to remark that it was indeed »the ideal communist abode because it is ultimately so transparent throughout«. Relatively few of the »non-initiated« visitors to the Maison de Verre come away calling it »beautiful« – although they may be amazed, seduced and intrigued (and occasionally even repulsed). Yet they nearly always find at least one feature – be it the bedroom closets or the bathtub-bookcase ensemble (ill. p. 146) – to be ingenious, practical or poetic, and often »before its time«.

Pierre Chareau's competence and ultimate mastery of his craft as a designer of furniture grew out of the years he spent working as a draughtsman for Waring & Gillow in Paris. In the course of his rise to the rank of master draughtsman, he participated on a great many different types of project, architectural commissions included. He came to know and work with a large number of cabinetmakers in Paris' celeb-

Die Dalsacesche Maison de Verre hat zu einer Vielzahl an Metaphern inspiriert, an denen sich nicht nur der klassische, archetypische Charakter des Hauses ablesen lassen, sondern auch seine revolutionären Qualitäten. Als das Haus fertig war, beschworen die Räume bei einigen Reportern Erinnerungen an die Innenhöfe des maurischen Andalusiens herauf, andere fühlten sich an ein Theater, ein Eskimoiglu (wegen der Glasbausteinfassade) oder gar an ein Schiff erinnert. Heute führen die eingebauten Möbel, die Schiebewände und Täfelungen, und die Besonderheiten der Räume (die visuelle Ungestörtheit zulassen, wobei jedoch der akustische Kontakt innerhalb der Wohnung erhalten bleibt) dazu, daß japanische Besucher das Haus als traditionell japanisch betrachten – und ein chinesischer Architekt bemerkte, daß es tatsächlich »die ideale Wohnung für Kommunisten ist, weil sie letzten Endes durch und durch transparent« sei. Relativ wenige »nicht eingeweihte« Besucher der Maison de Verre bezeichnen sie als »schön« – obwohl sie vielleicht überrascht, bezaubert und fasziniert sind (und es nur gelegentlich abstoßend finden). Und doch finden sie fast immer wenigstens eine Besonderheit – sei es nun der Einbauschrank im Schlafzimmer oder das Badewannen-Bücherschrank-Ensemble (Abb. S. 146) –, die genial, praktisch oder stimmungsvoll, und oft »vor ihrer Zeit« sind.

Pierre Chareau erlangte seine Kompetenz und seine höchst meisterhafte Geschicklichkeit als Möbeldesigner in den Jahren, in denen er als Zeichner bei Waring & Gillow in Paris arbeitete. Während seines Aufstiegs zum ersten Zeichner war er an sehr vielen verschiedenen Projekten beteiligt, auch an Bauaufträgen. Nach und nach lernte er eine Reihe von Möbeltischlern aus dem berühmten Pariser Möbelviertel an der Rue Faubourg St. Antoine kennen, mit denen er auch zusammenarbeitete; konkret war es die Firma Printz, auf die er schließlich zurückkam, als er seine eigene Firma gründete. Das detaillierteste Nachschlagewerk über Möbeltypen, -materialien, -formen und Stilrichtungen, das im England der Jahrhundertwende sehr verbreitet war, ist »Das englische Haus«, eine dreibändige Studie, die Hermann Muthesius (1904/05) zusammenstellte.[5] Der junge Chareau lernte wahrscheinlich nicht

(1904/5)[5]. Le jeune Chareau apprit probablement à réaliser de bonnes imitations de meubles Chippendale et Sheraton quand ce genre de style fut remis en vogue après 1900, ainsi qu'à prendre conscience du travail plus novateur de designers anglais tels que C.F.A. Voysey, M.H. Baillie Scott et même C.R. Mackintosh. Alors qu'il était employé d'une grande firme internationale à Paris, Chareau avait eu maintes occasions d'apprendre les méthodes d'artisanat et les nouvelles tendances françaises et étrangères. Il est facile d'imaginer comment Chareau a pu acquérir son penchant pour les conceptions solides et simples quand on sait qu'il a continuellement été exposé à la culture anglo-saxonne pendant plusieurs années. Il n'a jamais été prouvé que Chareau ait été influencé par des personnalités ou écoles de production spécifiques sur le continent, comme Josef Hoffmann ou les Wiener Werkstätte, par exemple, bien que l'on puisse certainement constater des affinités.

Les premiers dessins de Chareau représentent des meubles en bois dont la solidité, les proportions et le caractère massif reflètent l'influence britannique. La question de savoir comment un meuble touche le sol est présente d'un bout à l'autre de l'œuvre de Chareau. Bien que les pieds d'une armoire, d'une chaise ou d'une coiffeuse puissent être fuselés ou arrondis si l'on recherche l'élégance, le sens de la solidité et du poids proportionné aux matériaux employés n'est jamais sacrifié. En fait, quelques-unes des premières créations de Chareau ont un air presque rudimentaire (ce qui ne veut pas dire rustique); l'une de ces créations est le siège bas et ramassé destiné au bureau du docteur Dalsace (repr. p. 41) et exposé au Salon d'Automne de 1919, après que Chareau fut revenu du service militaire. L'épaisseur des pieds, l'angle légèrement malcommode des pieds arrière, le dossier haut et courbe aux coins arrondis, et le style des deux bras suggèrent un caractère primitif, aux allures de trône africain – ce qui n'était pas exceptionnel, vu la très forte influence de «l'art nègre» pendant cette période. Le siège est réalisé en acajou et couvert d'un placage en ébène de Macassar. Comme les deux petits sièges semblables, le sofa, le bureau et la commode, c'est là un curieux mélange de caractère primitif de la forme et d'élégance du finissage. Le lampadaire

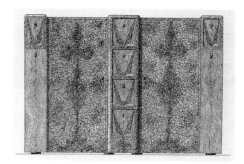

Lavis d'une armoire, vers 1925.
Ink drawing of armoire, c. 1925.
Tuschezeichnung eines Schrankes, um 1925.

rated furniture district along the rue Faubourg St. Antoine; indeed, it was to the firm of Printz that he was ultimately to return when he set up his own practice. The most detailed reference guide to the furniture types, materials, forms and styles prevalent in England at the turn of the century is »Das englische Haus« (The English House), a 3-volume study compiled by Hermann Muthesius (1904/5).[5] The young Chareau probably learned to produce good imitations of Chippendale and Sheraton furniture during the revival of such styles after 1900, as well as becoming aware of the more innovative work of English designers such as C.F.A. Voysey, M.H. Baillie Scott and even C.R. Mackintosh. Employed as he was with a large international firm in Paris, Chareau would have had every opportunity to learn both about changing methods of craftsmanship and new trends in France and abroad. It is easy to imagine how Chareau may have acquired his penchant for solidity and simplicity of conception from his continuous exposure over many years to Anglo-Saxon culture. Whether Chareau was ever influenced by specific personalities or schools of production on the Continent, such as Josef Hoffmann or the Wiener Werkstätte, for example, has never been documented, although affinities are surely discernible.

Chareau's earliest designs are items of wooden furniture whose strength, proportions and massiveness reflect a British influence. A concern which runs throughout

nur, wie man gute Imitationen von Chippendale- und Sheratonmöbeln herstellt, als diese Stile nach 1900 wiederauflebten, sondern er kannte auch die innovativere Arbeit der englischen Designer wie z.B. C.F.A. Voysey, M.H. Baillie Scott und sogar C.R. Mackintosh. Da er bei einer großen internationalen Firma in Paris beschäftigt war, hätte Chareau Gelegenheit gehabt, alles über die wechselnden Fertigungsmethoden beim Kunsthandwerk und über die neuen Trends in Frankreich und im Ausland zu erfahren. Man kann sich leicht vorstellen, wie Chareau zu seiner Vorliebe für stabile und einfache Entwürfe gelangte, nachdem er jahrelang den Einflüssen der angelsächsischen Kultur ausgesetzt war. Ob Chareau je von bestimmten Persönlichkeiten oder Produktionsschulen auf dem Kontinent, wie z.B. Josef Hoffmann oder die Wiener Werkstätten, beeinflußt wurde, ist nie dokumentiert worden, obwohl zweifelsohne Ähnlichkeiten erkennbar sind.

Bei Chareaus frühesten Entwürfen handelt es sich um Holzmöbel, deren Stärke, Proportionen und Massivität auf einen britischen Einfluß schließen lassen. Die Frage, wie ein Möbelstück den Boden berührt, zieht sich als ein roter Faden durch sein Werk. Auch wenn die Füße eines Schrankes, die Beine eines Stuhls oder einer Frisierkommode spitz zulaufend oder gerundet sein konnten, auf der Suche nach Eleganz opferte er nie seinen Sinn für Stabilität und Gewicht im Einklang mit den verwendeten Materialien. Einige seiner frühen Entwürfe haben tatsächlich so etwas wie ein rudimentäres (was nicht rustikal bedeutet) Aussehen; ein solcher Entwurf ist beispielsweise der hockerähnlich gestaltete Sessel für Dr. Dalsaces Büro (Abb. S. 41), der nach Chareaus Rückkehr aus dem Militärdienst 1919 in der Ausstellung Salon d'Automne ausgestellt worden war. Die dicken Beine, der leicht unbeholfene Winkel der hinteren Stuhlbeine, die hohe, nach hinten gebogene Rückenlehne mit ihren abgerundeten Ecken und die Neigung der Armlehnen verleihen ihm ein sehr einfach-schlichtes thronähnliches Aussehen (etwa das eines afrikanischen Thrones) – nichts Ungewöhnliches, in Anbetracht der äußerst starken Bedeutung der »l'art nègre« in dieser Periode. Der Sessel ist aus Mahagoni und mit einem Furnier aus Makassar-Ebenholz überzogen. Zusammen mit der Couch, dem Tisch und der Kommo-

(EB 6), qui fut photographié dans le bureau du docteur à peu près à la même époque (repr. p. 40), est fait de deux fins morceaux de bois, qui sont entaillés sur les côtés opposés et empiètent sur les côtés lisses, afin de pouvoir être ajustés verticalement avec un anneau. Le prédécesseur «primitif» de la célèbre lampe sculpturale surnommée «La Religieuse» (repr. p. 63) est surmonté d'un morceau d'albâtre triangulaire maintenu en place par des attaches métalliques.

Dans ces premières chaises et lampes de 1919–1920, il est en outre déjà possible de discerner quelques-unes des caractéristiques qui deviennent des leitmotive dans l'œuvre de Chareau. On trouve d'abord parmi celles-ci le concept de mobilité, soit d'une partie isolée soit d'un meuble en tant qu'ensemble. Le second thème est la transparence et la translucidité des matériaux dans une multitude de circonstances, allant de l'éclairage utilisant de l'albâtre semi-transparent ou des dalles de verre, à l'éclairage employant des écrans métalliques perforés. Le troisième thème est une sorte d'anthropomorphisme latent dans beaucoup de ses meubles – quoique pas tous –, une caractéristique qui n'est pas sans rapport avec la notion de mobilité, mais implique également des aspects formels. Les objets inanimés semblent parfois avoir leur propre «vie».

La façon dont Pierre Chareau absorbait les influences de son époque et de son milieu, transposant ces dernières à un autre niveau dans la mesure où le client et les programmes le permettaient, montre qu'il était un homme original ayant beaucoup de goût et d'humour. Des critiques tels que Waldemar George soulignèrent en 1923 qu'après des années de meubles et ensembles anglais qualifiés «de style» (historiciste), Chareau avait commencé à donner libre cours à ses propres «improvisations» en 1922.[6] Il attira l'attention sur le salon chinois, également connu sous le nom de Salon Coromandel (repr. p. 50), exécuté pour Madame Hélène Bernheim comme exemple d'improvisation sur un salon XVIIe. Un espace ovale, avec deux pièces adjacentes triangulaires, fut conçu pour abriter la collection de paravents chinois et autres objets de la cliente. Certains panneaux étaient fixés aux portes coulissantes donnant sur les pièces adjacentes. Malgré la vogue de l'art oriental, qui s'infiltre dans

Chareau's œuvre is the question of how a piece of furniture touches the floor. Although the feet of a cupboard, chair or dressing-table may be tapered or rounded in the search for elegance, the sense of firmness and weight commensurate with the materials employed is never sacrificed. Indeed, some of Chareau's early creations have an almost rudimentary (which does not imply rustic) air; one is the squatly-proportioned chair for Dr. Dalsace's office (ill. p. 41) exhibited in the 1919 Salon d'Automne, upon Chareau's return from military service. The thickness of the legs, the slightly awkward angle of the rear legs, the high, curved back with rounded corners, and the flair of the two arms suggests a primitive, even African throne-like character – something not unusual, given the very strong influence of »l'art nègre«in this period. The chair is built of mahogany and covered with a veneer of macassar ebony. Like its two smaller counterparts, together with the couch, the desk and the chest, it is a curious mixture of primitiveness in form and elegance in finishing. The floor lamp (EB6), photographed in the doctor's office about the same time (ill. p. 40), consists of two slender pieces of wood, notched on opposite sides and overlapping on the smooth sides so that they can be adjusted vertically with a ring. Surmounted by a triangular-shaped piece of alabaster, held in place by metal clips, it is the »primitive« predecessor of the more famous and sculptural lamp nicknamed »La Religieuse« (»The Nun«) (ill. p. 63).

In these first chairs and lamps of 1919–1920, moreover, it is already possible to discern some of the characteristics which go on to become leitmotifs in Chareau's œuvre. Foremost amongst these is the concept of mobility, whether of an individual part or a piece of furniture as a whole. A second theme is found in the transparency and translucence of materials in a multitude of circumstances, ranging from lighting using semi-transparent alabaster or glass bricks to that employing perforated metal screens. A third theme is a kind of latent anthropomorphism in many – albeit not all – of his pieces of furniture, a characteristic not unrelated to the notion of mobility, but one which also involves aspects of shape and form. Inanimate objects seem virtually to have a »life« of their own.

de ist der Sessel, ebenso wie seine beiden nicht ganz so großen Pendants, eine merkwürdige Mischung aus schlichter Form und eleganter Fertigstellung. Die Stehlampe (EB 6), die etwa zur selben Zeit im Büro des Doktors fotografiert worden war (Abb. S. 40), besteht aus zwei schlanken Holzstücken, die an den gegenüberliegenden Seiten eingekerbt sind und sich an den glatten Seiten überschneiden, so daß sie senkrecht mit einem Ring angepaßt werden können. Gekrönt von einem dreieckig geformten Stück Alabaster, das von Halterungen aus Metall gehalten wird, ist sie ein »primitiver« Vorgänger der berühmteren Skulpturlampe mit dem Spitznamen »La Religieuse« (»Die Nonne«; Abb. S. 63).

Überdies lassen sich bei diesen ersten Stühlen, Sesseln und Lampen von 1919–1920 bereits einige Merkmale erkennen, die später zu Leitmotiven in Chareaus Werk werden sollten. An erster Stelle finden wir hier die Konzeption der Veränderbarkeit, entweder eines Einzelteiles oder des Möbelstücks an sich. Ein zweites Thema ist die Transparenz und Lichtdurchlässigkeit der Materialien in vielen Bereichen; die Palette reicht hier von halbtransparentem Alabaster oder Glasbausteinen, die bei der Beleuchtung verwendet werden, bis hin zu Zwischenwänden aus Lochblech. Ein drittes Thema ist eine Art unterschwellige Vermenschlichung bei vielen, wenn auch nicht bei allen, seiner Möbelstücke – eine Eigentümlichkeit, die nicht ohne Beziehung zur Idee der Veränderbarkeit ist, sondern auch Aspekte der Struktur und Form beinhaltet. Leblose Objekte scheinen tatsächlich ein »Eigenleben« zu führen.

Pierre Chareau war ein Mann, der Originalität, Geschmack und einen ausgeprägten Sinn für Humor besaß. Dies zeigt sich in der Art und Weise, wie er die Strömungen seiner Epoche und seines Milieus in sich aufnahm und sie auf einer anderen Ebene umsetzte, soweit Kunden und Pläne dies zuließen. Frühe Kritiker seiner Arbeit, wie z. B. Waldemar George, wiesen bereits im Jahre 1923 darauf hin, daß Chareau, nachdem er sich jahrelang mit englischen Möbeln und Ensembles beschäftigt hatte, die er selbst als »de style« (stilecht) bezeichnete, im Jahre 1922 damit begonnen hatte, sich den eigenen »Improvisationen« hinzugeben.[6] Er verwies zum Beispiel auf den Salon Chinois (Chinesischer Salon), der

Bureau (MT876)
Desk (MT876)
Tisch (MT876)

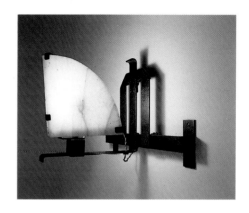

Applique
Wall lamp
Wandleuchte

That Pierre Chareau was a man who possessed considerable originality, taste and humour is revealed by the manner in which he absorbed influences of his era and his milieu, transposing these to another level as client and programme permitted. Early critics of his work, such as Waldemar George, pointed out in 1923 that Chareau, after years of English furnishings and ensembles which he terms »de style« (historicist), had in 1922 begun to indulge in »improvisations« of his own.[6] He pointed to the Salon Chinois (Chinese salon), also known as the Salon Coromandel (ill. p. 50), executed for Madame Hélène Bernheim as an example of an improvisation on a 17th-century drawing room. An oval space, with two adjacent triangular rooms, was conceived to house the client's collection of Chinese panel paintings and other objects. Some panels were fixed to the sliding doors to the side rooms. Despite the fashion in the early 1920s for Oriental art – something which permeates Chareau's own sensibility and taste – the Salon Coromandel displays the designer's reliance on sombre colours and formal »saturation« (W. George), and above all on mobility as a key element of the overall concept.

In 1920 the playwright Edmond Fleg, related to Annie Dalsace through his wife, Madeleine, had commissioned Chareau to decorate their apartment (ES750) on quai aux Fleurs (ill. p. 42), behind Notre-Dame cathedral. Principally an author of plays for the theatre, Fleg wrote one of the most perceptive early appreciations of the designer's work, identifying movement in the form of mobile furniture – i.e. furniture with moving elements or furniture which moved while attached to the building itself – as the hallmark of Chareau's inventiveness.[7] A determinant force behind the young decorator's thinking was undoubtedly the theatre – one of Chareau's longstanding passions, whereby the need to transform theatre space and the idea of space as a framework for human gestures, for presentation and representation exercised a strong influence on his designs.

Chareau analysed the implications of each human gesture, not simply in terms of its purpose and the effort required to accomplish a movement, but also for its grace and beauty. The lateral movement implied by sliding could also be solved by

la sensibilité et les goûts de Chareau au début des années vingt, le Salon Coromandel montre la préférence que le designer plaçait dans les couleurs sombres et la «saturation» formelle (W. George), et surtout dans la mobilité en tant qu'élément-clé du concept global.

En 1920, le dramaturge Edmond Fleg, apparenté à Annie Dalsace par sa femme Madeleine, avait chargé Chareau de décorer leur appartement (ES750) du quai aux Fleurs (repr. p. 42), derrière la cathédrale Notre-Dame. Fleg, qui écrivait principalement des pièces de théâtre, porta l'un des jugements les plus perspicaces sur l'œuvre du designer, identifiant le thème du mouvement dans ce mobilier mobile – par les éléments mobiles des ensembles se déplaçant tout en étant attachés au bâtiment lui-même – comme étant l'empreinte du génie inventif de Chareau[7]. Le théâtre – l'une des passions de longue date de Chareau – était sans aucun doute une force déterminante chez le jeune décorateur; le besoin de transformer l'espace théâtral et l'idée d'un espace polyfonctionnel, évolutif, un cadre pour les gestes humains, la présentation et la représentation, exerçent une grande influence sur ses dessins.

Chareau analysait les implications contenues dans chaque geste humain, non seulement sous l'angle du but visé et de l'effort requis pour accomplir un mouvement, mais aussi pour sa grâce et sa beauté. Le mouvement latéral impliqué par le glissement pouvait aussi être résolu par le

auch als »Salon Coromandel« (Abb. S. 50) bekannt war; Chareau hatte ihn für Madame Hélène Bernheim fertiggestellt und dabei ausgehend vom Beispiel eines Salons im 17. Jahrhundert improvisiert. Um die Sammlung chinesischer Tafelbilder und anderer Objekte der Kundin im Haus unterzubringen, entwarf er einen ovalen Raum mit zwei dreieckigen Nebenzimmern. Einige der Holztafeln wurden an den Schiebetüren der Nebenzimmer befestigt. Abgesehen davon, daß in den frühen zwanziger Jahren orientalische Kunst in Mode war – was dem Geschmack Chareaus entgegenkam –, zeigt der Salon Coromandel, wie der Designer auf düstere Farben und die »Durchsetzung der Form« (W. George) und vor allem auf die Veränderbarkeit als Schlüsselelement im Gesamtentwurf vertraute.

Im Jahre 1920 hatte der Bühnenautor Edmond Fleg, der seitens seiner Frau Madeleine mit Annie Dalsace verwandt war, Chareau mit der Dekoration seiner Wohnung (ES 750; Abb. S. 42), am Quai aux Fleurs, unweit der Kathedrale Notre-Dame gelegen, beauftragt. Fleg war zwar hauptsächlich Theaterautor für Theaterstücke, schrieb aber dennoch eine der positivsten und scharfsichtigsten frühen Kritiken über das Werk des Designers. Als Kennzeichen von Chareaus Erfindungsgabe bestimmte er Beweglichkeit in Form von beweglichen Möbeln – z. B. Möbel mit beweglichen Elementen oder verschiebbare Möbel, die am Gebäude selbst befestigt waren.[7] Das Denken des jungen Dekorateurs Chareau

pliage; ces gestes sont différents de ceux qu'il faut accomplir pour faire pivoter un objet. Il concevait des tables avec des éléments courbes, triangulaires, qui se développaient dans l'espace à partir d'un point fixe, définissant et redéfinissant l'espace occupé. C'est là le principe de la forme en éventail que Chareau utilisait pour des objets fixes comme les abat-jour en albâtre, et pour des bureaux ayant des rallonges mobiles comme des ailes. L'élégance est quelquefois accompagnée d'incommodité, comme dans le bureau avec plan incliné à chaque extrémité, d'où les objets ont tendance à glisser. Toutefois, Chareau dessina également quantité de meubles pour enfants qui étaient fort pratiques. Une table à langer pour bébé (repr. p. 59) conçue pour les Dalsace a des côtés qui se replient pour empêcher l'enfant de tomber. La mobilité devint la passion et la marque de Chareau, plus encore que pour tout autre designer de son époque.

Parmi les nombreuses préoccupations des peintres et sculpteurs d'avant-garde que fréquentait Chareau (et dont il collectionnait les œuvres), ce fut certainement la recherche des cubistes et des surréalistes qui eut l'impact le plus profond sur son œuvre. Outre ses relations intimes avec Jean Lurçat, son association de longue durée avec Jacques Lipchitz eut une importance particulière. On trouve non seulement dans l'œuvre de Chareau des échos des formes géométriques, anguleuses et courbes, des sculptures du Lipchitz du début des années vingt, mais les deux artistes montrent un intérêt parallèle pour la transparence de la forme et le mouvement naissant. Le critique Maurice Raynal, qui écrivit un article sur la sculpture de Lipchitz de la période 1922–24, nota que «la conception architectonique la plus lyriquement calculée évoque une poésie suivant la prosodie qui fait de ces compositions des mouvements d'une sûreté audacieuse, imprégnés de classicisme... Un module strict contrôle la plus hardie et pourtant la plus pure des lignes mélodieuses.» Il poursuit en observant que «c'est en 1925 que Jacques Lipchitz réalise une sculpture transparente»[8].

Ce fut également à cette époque que Lipchitz commença à faire des expériences avec la fonte, employant la technique du moulage à la cire perdue. Bien que les ori-

Détail de table basse (MB106)
Detail of low table (MB106)
Detail des niedrigen Tisches (MB106)

folding; these gestures are different from those required to pivot an object. He conceived tables with triangular, curved elements which developed in space from a fixed point, defining and redefining the space which they occupied. This is the principle of the fan shape, which Chareau would use both for stationary objects like the alabaster lampshades, and for desks which had movable, wing-like extensions. Elegance is sometimes accompanied by impracticality, as in the desk with an inclined plane at each end from which objects tend to slide. Chareau also designed a great deal of furniture for children's rooms, however, in which practicality prevailed. A changing table for a baby, conceived for the Dalsaces (ill. p. 59), has sides which fold up to prevent the child from rolling off. More than any other designer of his era, mobility became his passion and his trademark.

Of the many artistic concerns that preoccupied the avant-garde painters and sculptors whom Chareau frequented (and whose work he collected), it was certainly the research of the Cubists and the Surrealists which had the greatest impact upon his own work. In addition to his close relationship with Jean Lurçat, his longstanding association with Jacques Lipchitz

war zweifellos entscheidend vom Theater – eine seiner alten Leidenschaften – beeinflußt und zwar insofern, als daß die Notwendigkeit, Theaterraum umzugestalten, und die Idee des Raumes als Rahmen für menschliche Gesten wie Präsentationen oder Repräsentationen einen starken Einfluß auf seine Entwürfe ausübten.

Chareau analysierte die Bedeutung jeder einzelnen menschlichen Geste nicht nur einfach hinsichtlich ihrer Absicht und der Anstrengung, die erforderlich war, um eine Bewegung auszuführen, sondern auch mit Blick auf ihre Anmut und Schönheit. Die seitliche Bewegung beim Schieben ließe sich auch durch Falten erreichen; diese Gesten unterscheiden sich wiederum von jenen, die beim Drehen eines Objektes erforderlich sind. Chareau entwarf Tische mit dreieckigen, gebogenen Elementen, die sich von einem festen Punkt aus im Raum entfalteten, wobei sie den Raum, den sie einnahmen, abwechselnd in den Vorder- und in den Hintergrund stellten. Es handelt sich hierbei um das Prinzip der Fächerform, das Chareau sowohl bei seinen feststehenden Objekten wie den Lampenschirmen aus Alabaster als auch bei Tischen mit beweglichen, flügelähnlichen Verlängerungen benutzte. Das Elegante geht zeitweise mit dem Unpraktischen einher – wie etwa bei dem Tisch mit der schiefen Ebene, von dessen Enden die Gegenstände leicht herunterfallen. Chareau entwarf auch eine Vielzahl von Kindermöbeln, bei denen jedoch der Aspekt des Praktischen überwog. Bei einem für die Dalsaces entworfenen Wickeltisch (Abb. S. 59) ließen sich die Seiten hochklappen, damit das Baby nicht herunterfallen konnte. Mehr als bei jedem anderen Designer seiner Zeit wurde die Beweglichkeit für Chareau zur Leidenschaft und zugleich zu seinem Markenzeichen.

Die avantgardistischen Maler und Bildhauer, die Chareau häufig besuchte (und deren Werke er sammelte), waren auf der Suche nach neuen Ausdrucksmöglichkeiten. Zweifellos waren es jedoch die Arbeiten der Kubisten und Surrealisten, die die größte Bedeutung für sein Werk hatten. Außer seiner engen Beziehung zu Jean Lurçat, war seine langjährige Verbindung zu Jean Lipchitz noch von besonderer Bedeutung. In Chareaus Werk finden sich nicht nur genaue Nachahmungen der eckigen und gerundeten geometrischen Formen, die Lipchitz in den frühen zwanziger Jahren bei

Détail de bureau (MB673)
Detail of desk (MB673)
Detail des Schreibtisches (MB673)

gines précises de l'intérêt porté par Chareau au métal soient inconnues, c'est peut-être la sculpture de Lipchitz, le traitement des surfaces et les formes qu'il réalisait avec du métal qui alimentèrent la fascination qu'exerçaient sur Chareau les qualités du métal en tant que matériau pour meubles (et pour l'archictecture). Quoi qu'il en soit, il est certain que tout comme Lipchitz était aussi un «artisan», qui comprenait exactement les techniques employées par les hommes qui coulaient son œuvre en bronze ou en fer, Chareau avait également des connaissances approfondies des qualités des matériaux et des techniques employées par ses propres associés artisans.

Il était néanmoins audacieux d'employer de la pierre pour un abat-jour, au lieu d'utiliser du tissu, du papier ou du verre, par exemple, afin de profiter de sa translucidité et de produire une lumière diffuse. Sa combinaison de pierre et de métal, soit comme attaches d'éléments en pierre soit comme support en métal, était également osée. C'est dans le contexte de cette recherche et de cette expérimentation avec l'éclairage que Chareau rencontra et commença à travailler avec un homme qui allait modifier le cours de sa carrière de créateur: Louis Dalbet, un maître ferronnier qui fabriquait des objets d'art en métal. La forma-

was particularly significant. Not only are there echoes in Chareau's work of the geometric forms, angular and curved, of Lipchitz's sculpture of the early 1920s, but both artists demonstrate a parallel concern for the transparency of form and incipient movement. The critic Maurice Raynal, writing about Lipchitz's sculpture of the period 1922–24, noted that »the most lyrically calculated architectonic conception evokes a poetry following prosodies which make of these compositions movements of audacious sureness, impregnated with a classicism ... A strict module controls the most daring yet the purest of the melodious lines.« He goes on to observe that »it is in 1925 that Jacques Lipchitz achieves a transparent sculpture«.[8]

It was at this same time, too, that Lipchitz began to experiment with cast iron, using the lost wax technique. Although the precise origins of Chareau's own interest in metal are unknown, it may perhaps have been Lipchitz's sculpture, and the surface treatment and forms which he achieved in metal, which fuelled Chareau's fascination with the qualities of metal as a material for furniture (and for architecture). Whatever the case, it is certain that just as Lipchitz was also a »craftsman« who understood precisely the techniques employed by the men who cast his work in bronze or iron, so Chareau too had an intimate knowledge of the qualities of materials and techniques employed by his own artisan associates.

It was nevertheless daring indeed to employ stone for a lampshade, in place of cloth, paper or glass, for example, in order to take advantage of its translucent quality and produce a diffused light. Bold, too, was his combination of stone with metal, whether as clips holding pieces of stone together or as a metal stand. It was in the context of this research and experimentation with lighting that Chareau met and started working with a man who was to alter the course of his creative career – Louis Dalbet, a master ironsmith who manufactured art objects in metal. Dalbet's training as a »compagnon de la Tour de France«, his experience and imaginativeness, complemented Chareau's in extraordinary ways, beginning with the »simple« problems of lighting and other fixtures in 1922–23 and culminating in the Maison de Verre and numerous other interiors of the 1930s. What Dalbet brought to their col-

seinen Skulpturen verwendete. Beide Künstler zeigen gleichermaßen großes Interesse an der Transparenz der Form und Anfangsbewegung. Der Kritiker Maurice Raynal, der über Lipchitzs Bildhauerkunst in der Zeit von 1922–1924 schrieb, bemerkte: »...die äußerst lyrisch kalkulierte architektonische Gestaltung beschwört eine Poesie herauf, deren Metrik diese Kompositionen zu Bewegungen von kühner Sicherheit werden läßt, durchdrungen von einer gewissen Klassik (...) Ein strenges Modul kontrolliert die gewagteste, und zugleich reinste der wohlklingenden Linien,« Er bemerkt weiter, daß »es Jacques Lipchitz 1925 gelungen ist, eine transparente Skulptur zu schaffen«.[8]

Genau zu dieser Zeit begann Lipchitz, mit Gußeisen zu experimentieren, wobei er das Wachsausschmelzverfahren anwandte. Wie Chareau zu seinem eigenen Interesse an Metall kam, ist unbekannt. Wahrscheinlich faszinierte ihn jedoch Lipchitz' Skulptur sowie die Oberflächenbehandlung und die Formen, die dieser mit Metall erzielte, so sehr, daß sein eigenes Interesse an den Eigenschaften des Metalls als Material für Möbel (und als Baumaterial) erregt wurde. Genau so, wie Lipchitz auch »Handwerker« war, der genaue Kenntnisse besaß über die Techniken, welche die Arbeiter beim Guß seiner Werke in Bronze oder Eisen anwandten, so verfügte auch Chareau über genaueste Kenntnisse in bezug auf die Eigenschaften von Materialien und Techniken, welche die Kunsthandwerker, mit denen er zusammenarbeitete, verwandten.

Dennoch war es eigentlich gewagt, anstelle von beispielsweise Stoff, Papier oder Glas als Material für einen Lampenschirm Stein zu benutzen, um sich dessen lichtdurchlässigen Qualitäten zunutze zu machen und ein diffuses Licht zu schaffen. Ebenfalls kühn war seine Kombination von Stein mit Metall, entweder in Form von Halterungen, die Steinstücke zusammenhielten, oder als Metallständer. In dieser Phase des Erforschens von und Experimentierens mit Beleuchtungen begegnete Chareau einem Mann, mit dem er dann auch zusammenarbeitete und der die Richtung seiner kreativen Laufbahn ändern sollte. Es war der Meisterschmied Louis Dalbet, der Kunstobjekte aus Metall herstellte. Dalbets Ausbildung als »compagnon de la Tour de France«, seine Erfahrung und

tion de Dalbet comme «compagnon du Tour de France», son expérience et son esprit inventif, complétaient de façon extraordinaire les qualités de Chareau, en commençant par les «simples» problèmes relatifs à l'éclairage et à d'autres installations en 1922–23, et en finissant par la Maison de Verre et beaucoup d'autres intérieurs dans les années trente. Il ne faut pas sous-estimer l'apport de Dalbet dans leur collaboration.

Des exemples de cette collaboration furent exposés pour la première fois au Salon d'Automne en 1924. Chareau se mit ensuite à étendre son vocabulaire de créateur au métal (principalement le fer forgé au commencement), qu'il employa désormais non seulement pour l'éclairage, des écrans de cheminée et des jardinières, mais aussi pour des articles plus grands tels que chaises et tables, et finalement pour des bureaux et des bibliothèques. Le métal offrait des avantages considérables par rapport aux matériaux traditionnels comme le bois, surtout parce qu'il permettait d'atteindre le même degré ou un degré de solidité plus élevé pour une masse moindre. Il était désormais possible d'obtenir une apparence de légèreté et même d'élégance en utilisant des formes courbes. Les parties mobiles pouvaient être moins volumineuses, plus solides, et peut-être plus résistantes à l'usure.

Chareau n'était pas le premier à combiner le métal avec le bois, l'osier ou le verre; cela avait déjà été fait dans les années 1890 par les grandes figures de l'Art Nouveau, par Victor Horta en Belgique et d'autres encore – ce qui correspondait au temps de la jeunesse de notre designer. Même aujourd'hui, certains, comme l'éminent architecte hollandais Herman Hertzberger (qui décida, d'après lui, de devenir architecte après avoir visité la Maison de Verre), placent l'évolution de Chareau dans la tradition de l'Art Nouveau. Sa motivation pour utiliser le fer est toutefois loin du désir qu'avait l'Art Nouveau d'exploiter ses possibilités décoratives en le courbant afin de suggérer les formes organiques sinueuses trouvées dans la nature. Chareau préférait au contraire renoncer à tous les motifs purement décoratifs. C'étaient la sobriété et la grossièreté des rubans métalliques forgés et martelés, trempés dans la cire et teintés d'un noir terne dans l'atelier de Dalbet, qui attiraient sa sensibilité esthétique.

Jardinière en fer forgé (PF35)
Wrought-iron plant stand (PF35)
Schmiedeeiserner Blumenständer (PF35)

laborative effort should never be underestimated.

Examples of their common efforts were exhibited for the first time at the Salon d'Automne of 1924. Chareau subsequently began to extend and enlarge his design vocabulary to include metal (principally wrought iron at the outset), which he now employed not simply in lighting, fireplace screens and plant holders, but also in larger items such as chairs and tables, and eventually desks and bookcases. Metal offered considerable advantages over more traditional materials, such as wood, in particular because it allowed the same or an even greater degree of strength to be achieved for less mass. Hence it was possible to obtain an appearance of lightness and even elegance through the use of curved forms. Moving parts could be less voluminous, sturdier, and perhaps more resistant to wear.

Chareau was not the first to employ combinations of metal with wood, wicker or glass; this had already been done by the leading figures of Art Nouveau in the 1890s, by Victor Horta in Belgium and others – corresponding in time to the

Vorstellungskraft ergänzten die von Chareau auf besondere Weise; dies beginnt mit der Lösung der »einfachen« Probleme bei der Beleuchtung und anderen Inventarstücken in den Jahren 1922–23 und erreicht in der Maison de Verre und zahlreichen anderen Inneneinrichtungen der dreißiger Jahre ihren Höhepunkt.

Beispiele ihrer gemeinsamen Bemühungen wurden erstmals 1924 in der Ausstellung Salon d'Automne gezeigt. In der Folge begann Chareau seinen Designwortschatz zu erweitern, so daß dieser nun auch den Begriff Metall enthielt (am Anfang hauptsächlich Schmiedeeisen). Metall fand nicht nur bei der Beleuchtung, als Kamingitter oder Halter für Pflanzen, sondern ebenfalls bei größeren Stücken wie Tischen, Sesseln oder Stühlen, und schließlich bei Schreibtischen und Bücherregalen Verwendung. Gegenüber den herkömmlichen Materialien wie z. B. Holz bot Metall beträchtliche Vorteile, besonders weil es ermöglichte, mit weniger Masse den gleichen oder sogar einen höheren Grad an Stabilität zu erreichen. Daher war es möglich, durch die Verwendung geschwungener Formen ein leichtes und sogar elegantes Aussehen zu erhalten. Bewegliche Teile waren weniger voluminös, stabiler und vielleicht auch beständiger gegen Abnutzung.

Chareau war nicht der erste, der Metall und Holz oder Flechtwerk und Glas kombinierte: Dies hatten bereits in den neunziger Jahren des 19. Jahrhunderts führende Persönlichkeiten des Jugendstils, wie z. B. Victor Horta in Belgien, getan – zu einer Zeit also, in der Chareau noch ein Jugendlicher war. Auch heute gibt es noch einige, wie den hervorragenden niederländischen Architekten Herman Hertzberger (maßgeblich für seinen Entschluß, Architekt zu werden, war übrigens ein Besuch in der Maison de Verre), die Chareaus Entwürfe dem Jugendstil zurechnen würden. Chareaus Motivation, Schmiedeeisen zu verwenden, ist jedoch weit von dem Bestreben des Jugendstils entfernt, die dekorativen Möglichkeiten des Schmiedeeisens durch Biegen so auszunutzen, daß es an gewundene organische Formen erinnern läßt, wie sie in der Natur vorkommen. Ganz im Gegenteil Chareau verzichtete lieber auf alle rein dekorativen Motive. Seinem Sinn für Ästhetik entsprach eher die ausgesprochen grobe Qualität der geschmiede-

Le plus souvent, un meuble authentique conçu par Chareau et réalisé par Dalbet portait les traces des outils du maréchal-ferrant, tandis que les soudures et les têtes de vis restaient visibles.

L'équilibre et les proportions d'un objet créé par Chareau, l'emploi de formes rectilignes et orthogonales pour des supports ou des encadrements présentant des éléments en fer noirci, n'ont guère de points communs avec la sophistication de l'Art Nouveau ou le raffinement des laques japonaises, si populaires auprès de nombre de ses clients bourgeois dans les années vingt. Ils ont une plus grande affinité avec le vocabulaire formel issu du constructivisme russe et du mouvement hollandais De Stijl. Dans ses meubles contenant du métal, Chareau renonçait à la polychromie comme celle que l'on trouve dans les meubles de Rietveld, de Duiker ou de Bijvoët, préférant juxtaposer le fer à du bois, comme le sycomore, l'acajou, le frêne, le palissandre brésilien, ou à du cuir ou de l'osier. Quelquefois, comme dans le cas des coiffeuses, il combinait les pièces en plaqué argent ou en nickelé avec la fibre et les couleurs riches et subtiles du bois. De même, quand Chareau commença à faire des expériences avec le métal tubulaire pour les tabourets de bar du club de Beauvallon et les tables de l'hôtel de Tours en 1926–28 (repr. p. 88 et 92), il ne cherchait pas les formes curvilignes de Marcel Breuer au Bauhaus ou d'autres de ses contemporains français. Il se fiait plutôt aux tubes droits reliés avec des vis là où il le fallait, d'une façon franche et rationnelle.

Il peut paraître contradictoire que Chareau ait continué à dessiner des meubles avec vernis appliqués et à mettre en valeur le métal fait et assemblé à la main, tout en soutenant les membres avant-gardistes du CIAM qui préconisaient un plus grand emploi des produits fabriqués en usine. Quel raisonnement lui faisait donc suivre les techniques traditionnelles de l'ébénisterie et de la ferronnerie à un moment où la production mécanique et ses qualités esthétiques étaient considérées comme le but de l'avenir? Raymond Cogniat, qui écrivit un article sur le Salon d'Automne de 1929, remarque avec une ironie désabusée: «La table pour machines avec parties mobiles [note de l'auteur: le bureau conçu par Chareau pour Madame Dalsace, repr. p. 83] a une sorte d'aspect inéluctable dans

period of our designer's youth. There are some even today, like the outstanding Dutch architect Herman Hertzberger (whose own decision to become an architect was determined by a revelational visit to the Maison de Verre), who would place Chareau's development within the Art Nouveau tradition. His motivation in using wrought iron, however, is far removed from the Art Nouveau desire to exploit its decorative possibilities by curving it to suggest sinuous organic forms found in nature. On the contrary, Chareau favoured the renunciation of all purely decorative motifs. For him, it was the plain, coarse quality of the iron strips, forged and hammered, dipped in wax and given a dull black finish in Dalbet's workshop, which appealed to his aesthetic sensibility. More often than not, a genuine piece of furniture designed by Chareau and executed by Dalbet will carry the traces of the blacksmith's tools, the soldered joints and screw heads left visible.

The balance and proportions of a given object by Chareau, his use of rectilinear and orthogonal forms for supports or framing where the blackened iron elements are present, has little in common either with Art Nouveau or with the sophisticated Japanese lacquerwork so popular with many of his bourgeois clients in the 1920s. It has greater affinity with the vocabulary of forms emanating from Russian Constructivism and the de Stijl movement in Holland. In those of his pieces incorporating metal, Chareau abstained from polychromy of the sort found in the furniture of Rietveld or Duiker and Bijvoët, preferring instead to juxtapose the iron with wood, such as sycamore, mahogany, ash, or Brazilian rosewood, or with leather or wicker. Occasionally, as in the case of dressing-tables, he would combine silver-plated or nickel-plated components with the subtle, rich colours and grain of the wood. Similarly, when Chareau began experimenting with tubular metal for the bar stools at the Beauvallon Clubhouse and tables in the Hotel de Tours (ill. pp. 88, 92) in 1926–28, he was not seeking the curvilinear forms of Marcel Breuer at the Bauhaus or of others of his French contemporaries. Rather, he relied on straight tubes, joined where necessary with screws in a frank, rational fashion.

It may seem contradictory that Chareau

ten und getriebenen langen, schmalen Eisenstücke, die in seiner Werkstatt mit Wachs versiegelt und matt lackiert wurden. Ein echtes von Chareau entworfenes und von Dalbet gefertigtes Möbelstück weist meistens Spuren von Schmiedewerkzeugen auf, und die Lötstellen und Schraubenköpfe sind sichtbar.

Die ausgewogenen Proportionen von Chareaus Objekten und die Art, wie er geradlinige und rechtwinklige Formen als Stütze oder als Gestell für die geschwärzten Eisenelemente verwendet, hat weder viel mit dem Jugendstil gemeinsam noch mit den anspruchsvollen japanischen Lackarbeiten, die in den zwanziger Jahren bei vielen seiner bürgerlichen Kunden so beliebt waren. Sie besitzen mehr Ähnlichkeit mit dem Vokabular der Formen, das vom russischen Konstruktivismus und der De-Stijl-Bewegung in den Niederlanden herrührt. In den Stücken, in denen er Metall verwendet, verzichtet Chareau auf jene Vielfarbigkeit, wie sie in Möbeln von Rietveld oder Duiker und Bijvoët zu finden ist. Statt dessen kombinierte er lieber Eisen mit Holz (wie Sykomore, Mahagoni, Esche oder Palisander), Leder oder Flechtwerk. Hin und wieder (z. B. bei Frisierkommoden) kombinierte er versilberte oder vernickelte Teile mit den feinen und doch kräftigen Farben sowie der Maserung von Holz. Dementsprechend suchte er auch nicht die krummlinigen Formen eines Marcel Breuer im Bauhaus oder andere seiner französischen Zeitgenossen, als er begann mit Metallröhren zu experimentieren, beispielsweise für die Barhocker im Beauvallon-Klubhaus und für die Tische im Hotel de Tours 1926–1928 (Abb. S. 88 und 92). Er verließ sich eher auf gerade Röhren, die an den erforderlichen Stellen offen und zweckmäßig mit Schrauben verbunden wurden.

Es scheint ein Widerspruch zu sein, daß Chareau weiterhin Möbel mit aufgelegtem Furnier entwarf und auf die handgearbeitete und von Hand zusammengesetzte Qualität des Metalls besonderen Wert legte, während er gleichzeitig die avantgardistischen Mitglieder der CIAM unterstützte, die für mehr Verwendungsmöglichkeiten von fabrikmäßig hergestellten Erzeugnissen eintraten. Aus welchen Gründen folgte er den traditionellen Techniken der Möbeltischlerei und der Metallverarbeitung zu einem Zeitpunkt, als die maschinelle Her-

la simplicité de ses lignes. Elle rappelle une usine, et l'on est tenté de chercher sous la table pour voir s'il y a des courroies de transmission qui vont mettre en route le mécanisme tout entier.»[9] Il importe peu de savoir si c'est l'aspect nouveau et simple du bureau, qui combinait métal noir et cuir rougeâtre, ou bien son emploi avoué pour machines à écrire et à calculer qui provoqua les remarques humoristiques de Cogniat; ce qui importe est que le critique ne soit aucunement parvenu à distinguer le véritable objectif de l'artiste. Chareau ne produisait pas de modèles de meubles immédiatement destinés à la production de masse standardisée par l'industrie; il ne se livrait pas non plus à un exercice particulier d'invention de gadgets non conventionnels – que quelques critiques ultérieurs ont appelé son «bricolage». Il était profondément engagé dans la recherche, pris par sa collaboration avec Dalbet et d'autres: à savoir la recherche de la qualité de la conception grâce à l'association étroite d'artisanat novateur et de créativité intellectuelle et artistique à l'époque moderne.

should continue to design furniture with applied veneers and to emphasize the hand-worked, hand-assembled quality of the metal, while at the same time supporting the avant-garde members of CIAM who were advocating a greater use of factory-made products. What was his rationale in pursuing traditional techniques of cabinetmaking and metalworking at a moment in history when machine production and its aesthetic qualities were considered the goal of the future? Writing about the 1929 Salon d'Automne, Raymond Cogniat wryly remarked: »The table for machines with movable parts [Author's note: Chareau's desk for Mme. Dalsace, ill. p. 83] has a kind of inevitable look to it in the simplicity of its lines. It calls to mind a factory, and one is tempted to search under the table to see if there are transmission belts that are going to start up the whole mechanism.«[9] Whether it was the novel, unsophisticated look of the desk, combining black metal and reddish leather, or its declared use for typewriters and calculating machines, which provoked Cogniat's humorous remarks, is insignificant; what is important is the fact that the critic has utterly failed to recognize the artist's true objective. Chareau was neither producing models of furniture destined immediately for standardized mass production by industry, nor indulging in an idiosyncratic exercise of inventing unconventional gadgets – what some later critics have called his »bricolage« (»bits and pieces«). He was deeply committed to a quest, embodied in his collaborative approach with Dalbet and others: namely, a quest for quality of conception through the intimate association of innovative craftsmanship and intellectual, artistic creativity in the modern age.

stellung und die damit verbundenen ästhetischen Qualitäten als das Ziel der Zukunft angesehen wurden? Als Raymond Cogniat über die Ausstellung Salon d'Automne des Jahres 1929 schrieb, bemerkte er sarkastisch: »Der Maschinentisch mit beweglichen Teilen [Anm. d. Verf.: Chareaus Tisch für Frau Dalsace; Abb. S. 83] zieht durch die Einfachheit seiner Linien zwangsläufig die Blicke auf sich. Er erinnert an eine Fabrik, und man ist geneigt, unter dem Tisch nach dem Treibriemen zu suchen, der den ganzen Mechanismus in Gang setzt.«[9] Ob es nun das neuartige, eigentümliche Aussehen des Tisches, in dem schwarzes Metall mit rötlichem Leder kombiniert worden war, oder seine erklärte Verwendung für Schreib- und Rechenmaschinen war, was Cogniat zu seiner humorvollen Bemerkung reizte, ist nicht von Bedeutung; wichtig ist, daß der Kritiker die wahre Absicht des Künstlers völlig verkannt hat. Chareau produzierte weder bestimmte Möbelmodelle für die sofortige industrielle Massenproduktion noch widmete er sich der eigentümlichen Aufgabe des Erfindens unkonventioneller Apparate – was einige Kritiker später als »bricolage« (»Basteln«) bezeichneten. Bei seinen eigenen Entwürfen und in seiner Zusammenarbeit mit Dalbet und anderen hatte er nur ein Bestreben: nämlich den Entwürfen eine besondere Qualität durch die enge Verknüpfung von innovativem Können und intellektueller künstlerischer Kreativität im Modernen Zeitalter zu verleihen.

Installation au Salon d'Automne, 1923.
Installation at the Salon d'Automne, 1923.
Salon d'Automne, 1923.

La Maison de Verre

Comme l'a souligné Edmond Fleg dans son essai sur Chareau mentionné plus haut, «la première tâche du décorateur sera donc de démolir et de reconstruire». La Maison de Verre est le résultat d'une démolition – des façades côté cour et côté jardin d'un bâtiment XVIIIe – et l'insertion d'une nouvelle structure entre les murs mitoyens restant de part et d'autre, l'étage supérieur (qui avait été conservé) et le sol. C'est le chef-d'œuvre en raison duquel on se souviendra de Chareau, l'architecte et décorateur, et de ses deux collaborateurs, Louis Dalbet et Bernard Bijvoët. La nouvelle structure, faite de poteaux d'acier et de planchers en béton armé, était en place sous l'étage supérieur de l'ancien bâtiment en juillet 1928 – quelques semaines avant que le permis de construire la maison soit définitivement accordé par la Ville de Paris. Le Dr. Dalsace et sa famille ne purent s'installer dans la demeure et le cabinet médical achevés que quatre ans plus tard, en 1932, et ce pour quelque quatre millions de francs.

Dans son article original sur la maison écrit plus de trente ans après, l'architecte et critique Kenneth Frampton souleva la question qui a toujours rendu les visiteurs perplexes depuis lors: la Maison de Verre doit-elle être comprise comme maison au sens conventionnel ou comme meuble? Les briques de verre translucides qui composent la totalité des premier et second étages de la façade principale sur la cour, et une grande partie de la façade sur le jardin, ne confèrent guère un aspect traditionnel à l'édifice. Ils créent une membrane qui permet à une quantité extraordinaire de lumière naturelle de pénétrer dans les espaces intérieurs, tout en préservant l'intimité de ceux qui se trouvent à l'intérieur. La nuit, de grands projecteurs illuminent les façades depuis l'extérieur, projetant une chaude lumière diffuse vers l'intérieur sans compromettre l'intimité. Les briques de verre étaient déjà été utilisées depuis quelques années, aussi bien dans les bâtiments utilitaires, institutionnels et industriels que dans les pavillons d'exposition; en effet, l'Exposition Universelle de Paris en 1900 présenta un «palais lumineux» entièrement construit en verre que Chareau eut peut-être l'occasion de voir.[10] Jamais,

The House of Glass

As Edmond Fleg pointed out in his essay on Chareau mentioned earlier, »the first task of the decorator will be therefore to demolish and to rebuild«. The Maison de Verre is the result of a demolition – of the courtyard and garden façades of an 18th-century building – and the insertion of a new structure between the party walls that remained on either side, the top storey (which had to be preserved) and the ground. It is the masterpiece for which Chareau as an architect-designer, along with his two collaborators, Louis Dalbet and Bernard Bijvoët, is to be remembered. The new structure, of steel columns and reinforced concrete floors, was in place beneath the old upper storey by July 1928 – a few weeks before the final authorization to build the house was actually given by the City of Paris. Dr. Dalsace and his family were only able to move into the completed dwelling and offices four years later, in 1932, and at a cost of around four million francs.

In his seminal article about the house written more than 30 years later, the architect and critic Kenneth Frampton raised the question which has perplexed visitors ever since: is the Maison de Verre to be understood as a house in the conventional sense, or as a piece of furniture? The translucent glass bricks which compose the entire first and second storeys of the courtyard façade, and a large part of the garden façade as well, hardly give the edifice a traditional appearance. They create a membrane which allows an extraordinary amount of natural light to enter the interior spaces, while at the same time preserving privacy for those inside. At night, large spotlights illuminate the façades from the exterior, casting a warm diffuse light into the interior without compromising the privacy. Glass bricks had already been in use for some years, both in utilitarian, institutional and industrial buildings as well as in exhibition pavilions; indeed, the 1900 Exposition Universelle in Paris featured a »Palais lumineux« constructed entirely of glass, which Chareau may well have seen.[10] Never, however, had they been used so extensively for a prestigious edifice of this sort.

Hitherto unpublished drawings (ill. p. 30/

Das Haus aus Glas

Wie Edmond Fleg in seinem bereits erwähnten Essay über Chareau aufzeigte, »ist das Zerstören und Wiederaufbauen deshalb die erste Pflicht eines Innenarchitekten«. Die Maison de Verre ist das Ergebnis einer solchen Zerstörung – nämlich der Hof- und Gartenfassaden eines Gebäudes aus dem 18. Jahrhundert – und des Einfügens eines Neubaus zwischen den gemeinsamen Wänden, die auf beiden Seiten übriggeblieben waren, und zwischen Dachgeschoß (das erhalten bleiben mußte) und Erdgeschoß. Es ist ein Meisterstück, für das Chareau als Architekt-Designer zusammen mit seinen beiden Mitarbeitern, Louis Dalbet und Bernard Bijvoët, in Erinnerung bleiben wird. Das neue Gerüst aus Stahlpfeilern und verstärkten Betonböden stand bereits im Juli 1928 unter dem alten Obergeschoß – einige Wochen bevor die Stadt Paris die endgültige Baugenehmigung erteilte. Dr. Dalsace konnte mit seiner Familie jedoch erst vier Jahre später, im Jahr 1932, die fertigen Wohn- und Praxisräume beziehen. Die Baukosten beliefen sich auf rund vier Millionen französische Francs.

Der Architekt und Kritiker Kenneth Frampton schrieb dreißig Jahre nach Vollendung des Hauses einen originellen Artikel, in dem er eine Frage erhob, die seitdem die Besucher verwirrt: Ist die Maison de Verre nun als Haus im herkömmlichen Sinn zu verstehen oder als Möbelstück? Die lichtdurchlässigen Glasbausteine, aus denen die gesamte erste und zweite Etage der Hoffassade bestehen, und ein Großteil der Gartenfassade verleihen dem Gebäude wohl kaum ein herkömmliches Aussehen. Sie schaffen eine Membran, die außergewöhnlich viel natürliches Licht in die Räume des Hauses läßt und doch gleichzeitig die Privatsphäre seiner Bewohner wahrt. Nachts werden die Fassaden von außen mit großen Scheinwerfern erhellt, wodurch im Inneren ein warmes, diffuses Licht entsteht, ohne jedoch die Privatsphäre preiszugeben. Glasbausteine wurden schon seit einigen Jahren verwendet, sowohl bei zweckmäßigen institutionellen und industriellen Gebäuden als auch bei Ausstellungspavillons; tatsächlich war eine der Attraktionen der Pariser Exposition Universelle von 1900 das ganz aus Glas

cependant, ils n'avaient été autant utilisés pour un édifice aussi prestigieux.

Des plans jusqu'ici inédits (repr. p. 30/31), que Chareau soumit vraisemblablement en 1927 pour appuyer sa demande de permis de construire, montrent que la maison Dalsace était à l'origine conçue de manière plus conventionnelle. Chareau ébaucha effectivement deux projets préliminaires pour la Maison de Verre, indiquant ainsi qu'il avait déjà un concept d'ensemble pour la maison et n'improvisait pas complètement depuis le début. La structure fut apparemment projetée d'abord avec des colonnes en béton armé plutôt qu'en acier. Pour les vastes surfaces vitrées des deux façades, diverses formes de verre transparent et dépoli étaient prévues. Chareau raconta plus tard au cours d'une interview qu'il avait fait des expériences avec l'acier, mais l'avait finalement rejeté pour employer des dalles de verre.[11]

Le pourquoi du choix des dalles de verre est une question légitime et fut soulevée en 1931 par la presse populaire locale et étrangère alors que la maison était presque terminée. L'une des nombreuses réponses possibles est que le client, un docteur, voulait que son cabinet de consultation et son laboratoire situés au rez-de-chaussée soient inondés de lumière naturelle, tout en conservant un maximum d'intimité pour ses patients. Deuxièmement, l'architecte était lui-même fortement influencé par une tendance idéologique de la pensée architecturale française qui mettait en vedette l'hygiène physique et mentale; quel meilleur choix, donc, qu'un matériau relativement solide, durable, demandant peu d'entretien ou de nettoyage à l'extérieur et offrant un maximum de lumière à l'intérieur? De plus, la lumière diffuse ou réfléchie plutôt que la lumière directe (soit artificielle soit naturelle) faisait depuis longtemps partie des préférences de Chareau quand il dessinait des intérieurs.

Il existe certainement beaucoup d'autres explications au fait que Chareau ait choisi des dalles de verre. Mais les vastes surfaces vitrées – qui contenaient peu de fenêtres ouvrant réellement – provoquèrent une autre question de la part du public et des autorités municipales. La ventilation de l'intérieur était en cause, et la solution adoptée était un système mécanique qui aspirait l'air à l'extérieur, le filtrait, le réchauffait en hiver et le rafraîchissait en été,

31), which Chareau must have submitted in 1927 as part of his planning application, reveal that the Dalsace house was initially conceived in more conventional terms. Chareau in fact drew up two different preliminary proposals for the Maison de Verre, indicating that he had already decided an overall concept for the house and did not improvise totally from the outset. The structure was apparently first projected with reinforced concrete rather than steel columns, and various forms of transparent and frosted (»dépoli«) glass were foreseen for the vast areas of glazing on both façades. Chareau himself said later in an interview that he had experimented with the latter, but subsequently rejected it in favour of glass bricks.[11]

The question of why the choice of glass bricks is a legitimate one, and was being raised even in 1931, as the house was nearing completion, by the popular press both at home and abroad. One of the many possible answers is that the client, a doctor, wanted his consulting rooms and laboratory on the ground floor to be inundated with natural light, while at the same time preserving maximum privacy for his patients. Secondly, the architect himself was strongly influenced by an ideological trend in French architectural thinking that emphasized physical and mental hygiene; what better choice, then, than a relatively sturdy, durable material needing little maintenance or cleaning on the exterior and offering maximum illumination inside? Moreover, diffuse or reflected light rather than direct lighting (whether artificial or natural) had long been one of Chareau's preferences when designing interiors.

There are undoubtedly many other explanations for Chareau's choice of glass. But the large glazed surfaces – which contained few windows that actually opened – provoked another question from both the public and the municipal authorities. At issue was the ventilation of the interior, and the solution adopted was a mechanical system which took in air from outside, filtered and heated it in winter and cooled it in summer, and then pumped it throughout the Maison de Verre by means of ducts under the floors. Dr. Dalsace himself signed a letter to the Parisian building authorities confirming the norms that would be met for renewal of air inside his future home.

konstruierte »Palais lumineux«, das Chareau möglicherweise auch gesehen hatte.[10] Glasbausteine waren jedoch bislang nie so umfassend für ein derartiges Renommiergebäude verwendet worden.

Aus bislang unveröffentlichten Zeichnungen (Abb. S. 30/31), die Chareau wahrscheinlich als Teil seiner Bewerbungspläne im Jahre 1927 unterbreitet hatte, geht hervor, daß der Entwurf für das Dalsace-Haus ursprünglich weitaus konventioneller war. Genaugenommen entwarf er zwei verschiedene vorläufige Vorschläge für die Maison de Verre, was darauf schließen läßt, daß er bereits eine Gesamtkonzeption des Hauses erstellt hatte und nicht gleich von Anfang an gänzlich improvisierte. Anscheinend war das Gebäude zuerst eher mit verstärktem Beton als mit Stahlpfeilern entworfen worden, und für die riesigen zu verglasenden Flächen auf beiden Seiten der Fassade waren verschiedene Arten von transparentem Glas und Milchglas (»dépoli«) vorgesehen. Chareau selbst sagte später einmal in einem Interview, daß er mit letzterem zwar experimentiert hätte, sich aber anschließend doch für Glasbausteine entschieden habe.[11]

Die Frage, warum er Glasbausteine wählte, scheint berechtigt und wurde 1931, als das Haus sich seiner Fertigstellung näherte, auch von der allgemeinen Presse im In- und Ausland erhoben. Eine der vielen möglichen Antworten auf diese Frage ist, daß der Kunde, ein Arzt, seine Sprechzimmer und sein Labor im Erdgeschoß haben wollte, damit die Räume mit natürlichem Licht überflutet werden sollten, während gleichzeitig ein Höchstmaß an Ungestörtheit für seine Patienten gewahrt wurde. Zum zweiten war der Architekt selbst von einem starken ideologischen Trend im französischen Architekturdenken beeinflußt, der besonderen Wert auf die Reinheit von Körper und Geist legte. Was war in dem Falle also besser als ein relativ stabiles, langlebiges Material, das mit einem Minimum an Wartung und Pflege von außen ein Maximum an Beleuchtung im Inneren bot? Außerdem bevorzugte Chareau lange Zeit bei seinen Entwürfen für Inneneinrichtungen eher diffuses oder reflektiertes Licht als direkte Beleuchtung.

Zweifellos gibt es noch andere Erklärungen dafür, daß Chareau Glas als Material wählte. Aber die großen verglasten Flä-

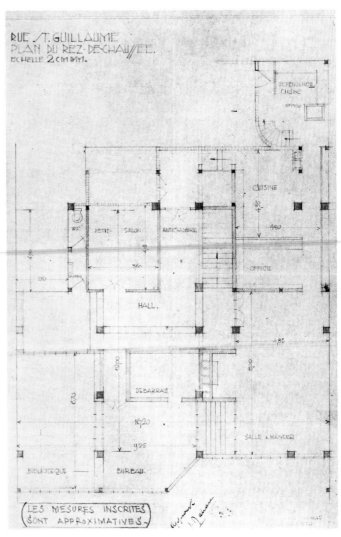

Projet préliminaire I
Plan du rez-de-chaussée, vers 1927
Plan du premier étage, 1927
Plan du deuxième étage, 1928

Preliminary project I
Ground floor plan, c. 1927
First floor plan, 1927
Second floor plan, 1927

Vorentwurf I
Grundriß des Erdgeschosses, um 1927
Grundriß der ersten Etage, 1927
Grundriß der zweiten Etage, 1927

Projet préliminaire II
Plan du rez-de-chaussée, 1928
Plan du premier étage, 1928
Plan du deuxième étage, 1928

Preliminary project II
Ground floor plan, 1928
First floor plan, 1928
Second floor plan, 1928

Vorentwurf II
Grundriß des Erdgeschosses, 1928
Grundriß der ersten Etage, 1928
Grundriß der zweiten Etage, 1928

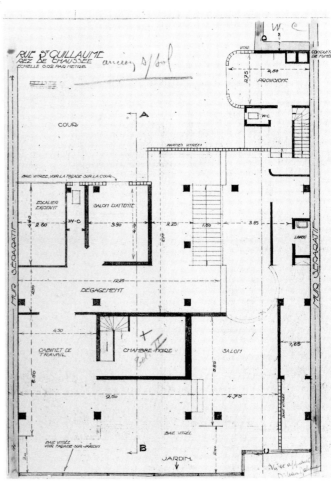

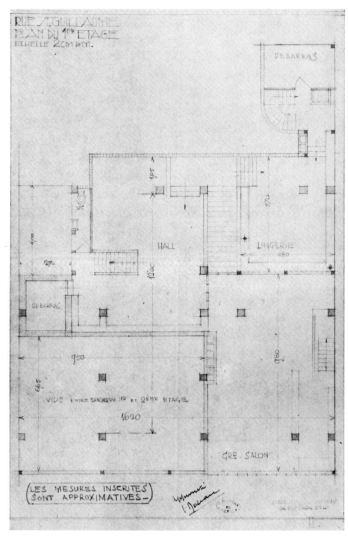

RUE St GUILLAUME
PLAN DU 1er ETAGE
ECHELLE 2 CM P.M.

DEBARRAS

HALL

LINGERIE

DEBARRAS

VIDE ENTRE PLANCHER DU 1er ET 2ème ETAGE

GD. SALON

LES MESURES INSCRITES
SONT APPROXIMATIVES —

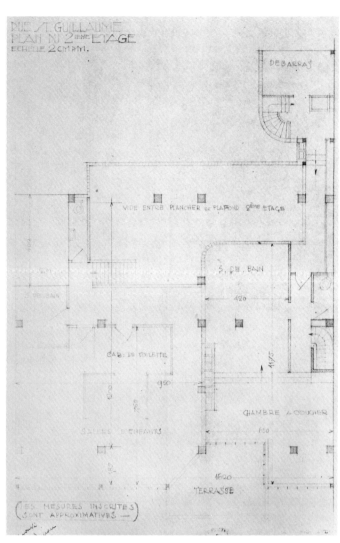

RUE St GUILLAUME
PLAN DU 2ème ETAGE
ECHELLE 2 CM P.M.

DEBARRAS

VIDE ENTRE PLANCHER ET PLAFOND 2ème ETAGE

S. DE BAIN

CAB. DE TOILETTE

CHAMBRE A COUCHER

SALLE D'ENFANTS

TERRASSE

LES MESURES INSCRITES
SONT APPROXIMATIVES —

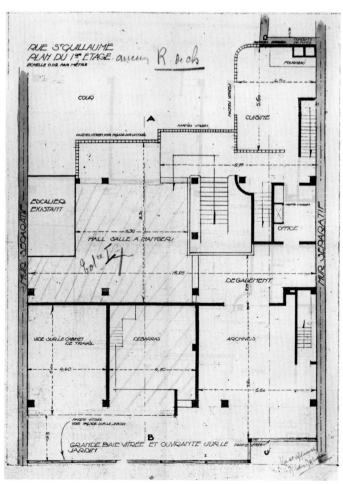

RUE St GUILLAUME
PLAN DU 1er ETAGE
ECHELLE 0.02 PAR METRE

COUR

CUISINE

ESCALIER
EXISTANT

OFFICE

HALL SALLE A MANGER

DEGAGEMENT

VIDE SUR LE CABINET
DE TRAVAIL

DEBARRAS

ARCHIVES

GRANDE BAIE VITRÉE ET OUVRANTE SUR LE JARDIN

MUR SEPARATIF

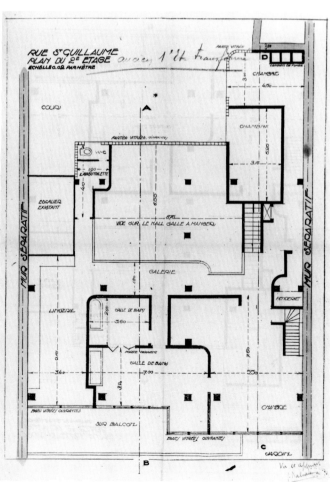

RUE St GUILLAUME
PLAN DU 2e ETAGE
ECHELLE 0.02 AU METRE

CHAMBRE

COUR

CHAMBRE

ESCALIER
EXISTANT

WC

LAVABO TOILETTE

VIDE SUR LE HALL SALLE A MANGER

GALERIE

LINGERIE

SALLE DE BAIN

PENDERIE

SALLE DE BAIN

CHAMBRE

SUR BALCON

MUR SEPARATIF

puis le distribuait dans la Maison de Verre au moyen de conduites sous les sols. Le Dr. Dalsace signa une lettre adressée aux services parisiens de la construction confirmant les normes qui seraient appliquées pour le renouvellement de l'air dans sa future maison.

Dans la seconde série de plans, probablement soumise en 1928, la disposition des espaces intérieurs est plus proche de ce qui a vraiment été exécuté et montre une distribution de pièces (à l'exception de celles des enfants) plus pratique – la salle de bains ne donne plus sur le salon – ainsi qu'une relation plus judicieuse entre les espaces. Bien que cela ne soit pas prouvé, il se pourrait bien que Bijvoët, le jeune assistant néerlandais de Chareau, ait eu une influence positive sur l'évolution des plans à ce stade.

Abandonnons pour le moment la question relative à la classification de la Maison de Verre – comme maison ou comme meuble –, et contentons nous de dire que la «méthode» qu'employa Chareau pour dessiner les espaces intérieurs une fois que les deux murs extérieurs furent installés était la même que celle qu'il employait pour ses meubles. Les Dalsace vivaient à quelques centaines de mètres seulement du site et venaient fréquemment, sinon quotidiennement (surtout Madame Dalsace), pour concevoir, discuter et modifier les installations avec Chareau, Bijvoët et Dalbet. Ce dernier partait avec des instructions et peut-être un croquis ou deux, et revenait avec des prototypes, souvent sous forme de maquettes grandeur nature. Une soigneuse analyse ultérieure faite par l'architecte et historien Bernard Bauchet a révélé qu'un module de 91 cm guidait à l'époque une grande partie de leur travail, particulièrement dans le cas des nombreux types de panneaux utilisés pour diviser les espaces horizontaux.[12]

Aucun des plans préliminaires ne montre l'introduction de meubles encastrés, soit fixes soit mobiles. Les murs intérieurs, qui ne sont pas portants, sont minces et placés indépendamment des colonnes portantes, d'une manière tout à fait similaire aux villas créées par Le Corbusier à la même époque. Manifestement, donc, ce fut seulement après que les solutions pour les murs extérieurs, le chauffage et la ventilation de l'intérieur eurent été adoptées que Chareau porta son attention sur la ba-

In Chareau's second set of plans, probably submitted in 1928, the disposition of interior spaces is much closer to what was actually executed, revealing shapes of rooms (except for those of the children) that are more practical – the bathroom no longer overlooks the salon – and a linkage of spaces that is more judicious. Although we have no evidence, it is not unlikely that Chareau's young assistant, Bijvoët, may have had a positive influence on the evolution of the plans at this stage.

Leaving aside for the moment our earlier question of how the Maison de Verre should be classified – as a house or a piece of furniture, it is true to say that the »method« by which Chareau proceeded to design the interior spaces once the two outer walls were installed was much the same as the method he employed for his furniture. The Dalsaces lived only a few hundred metres away from the site, and came frequently, if not daily (especially Mme Dalsace), to plan, discuss and modify the installations with Chareau, Bijvoët and Dalbet. This last would leave with instructions and perhaps a sketch or two, and return with phototypes often in the form of full-scale models. Careful subsequent analysis by architect-historian Bernard Bauchet has shown that a module of 91 centimetres guided much of their work at the time, particularly in the case of the numerous types of panels that were used to divide horizontal spaces.[12]

None of the preliminary plans show the inclusion of built-in furniture, either stationary or mobile. The interior walls, which are non-bearing, are thin and set independently of the supporting columns, in a manner quite similar to Le Corbusier's villas of the period. Clearly, therefore, it was not until the solutions for the outer walls and for the heating and ventilation of the interior had been adopted that Chareau turned his attention to the bookcase balustrade and to the cabinets forming the partitions in the main salon and dining area. Although the mobile bookcases shown in one of the three remaining de Stijl-like perspectives were not in fact executed, Chareau nevertheless succeeded in introducing mobility in the unique solution developed for the bookcases next to the main stairs, in the second-floor corridor and in the bathtub-bookcase ensemble of the daughter's bedroom, whose shelves were

chen – die nur wenige Fenster besaßen, die sich tatsächlich öffnen ließen – warfen in der Öffentlichkeit und bei den städtischen Behörden eine andere strittige Frage auf, nämlich die nach der Belüftung im Inneren des Hauses. Die Lösung bestand in einem mechanischen System, das die Luft von außen ansog, filterte, im Winter erwärmte und im Sommer kühlte und sie durch Rohre im Fußboden durch die ganze Maison de Verre pumpte. Dr. Dalsace selbst unterschrieb einen Brief an die Pariser Baubehörden, in dem er die Einhaltung der Normen zur Lufterneuerung in seinem zukünftigen Haus bestätigte.

In Chareaus zweitem Bauplan, den er wahrscheinlich im Jahre 1928 unterbreitete, entspricht die Raumaufteilung schon eher ihrer endgültigen Anordnung. Der zweite Entwurf zeigt Raumformen (mit Ausnahme der Kinderzimmer), die praktischer sind – man kann z. B. vom Badezimmer nicht mehr hinunter auf den Salon sehen –, und rationale Raumverbindungen. Obwohl wir keinen Beweis dafür haben, ist es wahrscheinlich, daß Chareaus junger Assistent, Bijvoët, in diesem Stadium vielleicht einen positiven Einfluß auf die Entwicklung der Pläne hatte.

Wenn wir für einen Moment unsere frühere Frage außer acht lassen, wie die Maison de Verre eingestuft werden sollte – als Haus oder als Möbelstück –, so läßt sich wirklich sagen, daß die »method« mit der Chareau bei der Gestaltung der Innenräume begann, sobald die beiden Außenwände hochgezogen waren, ungefähr die gleiche Methode war, die er bei seinen Möbeln anwandte. Die Dalsaces lebten nur wenige hundert Meter von der Baustelle entfernt und kamen häufig vorbei, häufig sogar täglich (insbesondere Frau Dalsace), um die Innengestaltung mit Chareau, Bijvoët und Dalbet zu planen, zu diskutieren und abzuändern. Die beiden letztgenannten verließen die Baustelle dann mit Anweisungen und vielleicht ein oder zwei Skizzen und kamen mit Phototypien, oft in Form von Modellen in Originalgröße, zurück. Spätere, sorgfältige Analysen des Architekturhistorikers Bernard Bauchet bewiesen, daß ein Modul von 91 Zentimetern damals einen Großteil ihrer Arbeit bestimmte, besonders bei den vielen verschiedenen Paneelen, die zur horizontalen Teilung der Räume verwendet wurden.[12]

Keiner der Vorentwürfe sieht Einbaumöbel

lustrade-bibliothèque et les meubles formant cloison dans le salon principal et l'espace repas. Bien que la bibliothèque mobile montrée dans l'une des trois perspectives restantes aux allures De Stijl n'ait pas été réalisée, Chareau parvint néanmoins à introduire la mobilité dans l'unique solution mise au point pour la bibliothèque proche de l'escalier principal, dans le couloir du second étage et dans l'ensemble baignoire-bibliothèque de la chambre de la fille de la maison, dont les étagères étaient des plateaux de métal et de verre armé que l'on pouvait sortir. Il dessina également des bibliothèques, les unes suspendues à des glissières au plafond (petit salon), d'autres couvrant un mur entier (grand salon), et marquant une double profondeur avec un arrangement à deux étages; une échelle mobile spéciale permettait d'accéder aux niveaux supérieurs.

Chareau avait beaucoup de points communs avec l'architecte autrichien Adolf Loos cité plus haut. Il était non seulement apparemment d'accord avec Loos sur le fait que les fenêtres étaient fondamentalement nécessaires pour faire entrer la lumière plus que pour regarder dehors (d'où, seul le verre translucide était requis), mais aussi avec l'observation que fit Loos en 1924, et selon laquelle: «Il est même moins moderne de conserver des vêtements dans des «armoires» qui se présentent comme des pièces d'apparat. Songeons y: une armoire n'est rien d'autre qu'une sorte d'écrin pour un ornement précieux.»[13] Les armoires conçues pour le second étage sont précisément cela: des boîtes de métal peintes en noir qui constituent un «mur» entre le couloir et les chambres. Elles peuvent être ouvertes des deux côtés, avec des portes à deux battants – l'une en métal courbe, l'autre en bois – du côté de la chambre pour offrir un espace de rangement supplémentaire. De plus, si l'on ouvre toutes les portes de l'armoire en même temps (ce qui est peu probable d'un point de vue pratique, il est vrai), il s'ensuit une interpénétration complète d'espaces architecturaux depuis les chambres et la salle de bains principale au travers du salon et la façade en dalles de verre sur le devant de la maison.

La maison laisse même voir des espaces dans les espaces créés au moyen d'éléments mobiles fixés à l'architecture – une fois encore, un exposé de l'un des thèmes

designed as metal and reinforced glass trays which could be lifted out. He also designed bookcases suspended from rails near the ceiling (small salon), others covering an entire wall (large salon) and featuring a double-depth, two-tier arrangement with a special mobile ladder for access to upper levels.

Chareau had a great deal in common with the Austrian architect Adolf Loos cited earlier. Not only did he apparently agree with Loos that windows were basically necessary for letting light in rather than for gazing out of (and hence only translucent glass was required), but also with Loos's observation of 1924 that: »It is even less modern to keep clothes in closets («armoires«) which offer themselves as showpieces. Imagine this: a closet is nothing more than a kind of case for a precious ornament.«[13] The closets conceived for the second floor are precisely this: metal cases painted black that constitute a »wall« between the corridor and the bedrooms. They can be opened from both sides, with double doors – one of curved metal, one of wood – on the bedroom side to provide additional storage space. Moreover, opening all the cupboard doors at the same time (admittedly unlikely from a practical point of view) results in a complete interpenetration of architectural spaces from bedrooms and master bathroom through to the salon and glass brick façade at the front of the house. The house even reveals spaces within spaces, created by means of mobile elements fixed to the architecture – again a statement of one of the enduring themes of Chareau's work. Pertinent examples include the movable screens that seclude the washbasin and bidet in each of the two children's bedrooms. Descendants of the traditional screens behind which people dressed and undressed, these creations of metal tubes and perforated sheet-metal are perfectly balanced on rollers and can be moved quietly and effortlessly as need dictates. They transform the bedroom space in an efficacious, subtle, even theatrical manner; they compartmentalize without truly dividing the space, for they remain transparent. These moving screens epitomize the collaboration between Chareau the artist-intellectual and Dalbet the ingenious master craftsman. Like the bookcase and bathtub unit, they transcend the level of mere domestic fixture and become part

vor, weder feststehende noch bewegliche. Die nichttragenden Innenwände sind dünn und unabhängig von den Stützpfeilern gesetzt, ganz ähnlich wie auch in den damaligen Villen Le Corbusiers. Ohne Zweifel wandte Chareau seine Aufmerksamkeit der Bücherschrankballustrade und den Schränken, die den Hauptsalon vom Eßbereich trennten, erst dann zu, als Lösungen für die Probleme Außenwände, Heizung und Belüftung der Innenräume gefunden waren. Obwohl die beweglichen Bücherregale, die in einer der drei verbleibenden De-Stijl-ähnlichen Perspektiven gezeigt werden, nicht wirklich angefertigt wurden, gelang es Chareau trotzdem, bewegliche Bücherregale zu gestalten. Es sind dies die Bücherregale, die jeweils auch als einzig mögliche Lösung entworfen wurden: Sie befinden sich neben der Haupttreppe, im Flur des zweiten Geschosses und in dem Badewannen-Bücherregal-Ensemble im Schlafzimmer der Tochter, bei letzterem wurden die Borde als herausnehmbare Tabletts aus Metall und verstärktem Glas gestaltet. Chareau entwarf auch Bücherregale, die an Schienen an der Decke aufgehängt waren (kleiner Salon), eine ganze Wand einnahmen (großer Salon), und eine doppelt tiefe, zweistufige Kombination mit einer speziellen beweglichen Leiter für den Zugang zu den oberen Ebenen.

Chareau hatte viel gemeinsam mit dem bereits zitierten österreichischen Architekten Adolf Loos. Anscheinend stimmte er mit Loos nicht nur darin überein, daß Fenster im Grunde eher notwendig waren, um Licht in den Raum zu lassen als zum Hinaussehen (und deshalb sei nur lichtdurchlässiges Glas erforderlich), sondern auch mit Loos' Beobachtung aus dem Jahr 1924: »Es ist sogar weniger modern, Wäsche in Schränken (»armoires«) aufzubewahren, die sich selbst als Schaustück anbieten. Stellen sie sich vor: Ein Schrank ist nichts weiter als eine Art Behälter für ein wertvolles Ornament.«[13] Die Schränke, die für das zweite Geschoß entworfen wurden, sind genau das: schwarz gestrichene Metallbehälter, die eine »Mauer« zwischen dem Flur und den Schlafzimmern bilden. Sie lassen sich von beiden Seiten öffnen, wobei die Doppeltüren – eine aus gewölbtem Metall, eine aus Holz – auf der Schlafzimmerseite zusätzlichen Stauraum bieten. Ein gleichzeitiges Öffnen aller

permanents de l'œuvre de Chareau. Les écrans mobiles isolant le lavabo et le bidet dans chacune des deux chambres d'enfants en sont des exemples judicieux. En tant que successeurs des paravents traditionnels derrière lesquels les gens s'habillaient et se déshabillaient, ces créations de tube métallique et de tôle de métal perforé sont parfaitement équilibrées sur des roulettes et peuvent être déplacées silencieusement et sans effort selon les besoins. Elles transforment l'espace de la chambre d'une façon efficace, subtile, voire théâtrale; elles compartimentent l'espace sans réellement le diviser, car elles restent transparentes. Ces écrans mobiles incarnent la collaboration entre Chareau, l'artiste et l'intellectuel, et Dalbet, l'ingénieux maître artisan. Comme l'ensemble bibliothèque-baignoire, ils transcendent le niveau de la simple installation domestique et deviennent partie de la poésie surréaliste de Chareau dans la Maison de Verre. Notre perception sensorielle est sans cesse perturbée dans ces espaces par l'incongruité des choses – que Rimbaud appelait «le dérangement de nos sens».

Chareau écrivit un jour: «Seules les nouvelles images excitent nos émotions!» Mais les nouveautés inventives de ses installations – quelquefois déconcertantes, quelquefois magiquement évocatrices – dans la Maison de Verre représentent néanmoins une dimension secondaire, seulement invoquée une fois que la solution rationnelle, logique étayant la maison avait été trouvée. «L'architecture est un art social», disait Chareau. «L'architecte peut seulement créer s'il écoute et comprend les voix des millions d'hommes, s'il souffre comme eux, s'il lutte avec eux pour les sauver. Il emploie le fer qu'ils ont forgé, il les guide vers le futur parce qu'il sait ce qui appartient au passé.»[14]

Bien qu'il soit fascinant de comparer la Maison de Verre avec d'autres bâtiments des contemporains de Chareau afin de vérifier sa juste place dans le mouvement moderne, on est inévitablement ramené à la conviction qu'elle est absolument unique. Il est néanmoins indiscutable que Chareau connaissait l'œuvre de Frank Lloyd Wright, par exemple, grâce à des publications et à des collègues tels que son propre assistant, Bernard Bijvoët, et la Maison de Verre a plus de points communs avec les «textile block houses» de Wright

«Construction avec blocs en texture» en Californie, par Frank Lloyd Wright, 1922/23.

»Textile block« house in California, by Frank Lloyd Wright, 1922/23.

»Gewebe-Blockhaus« von Frank Lloyd Wright in Kalifornien, 1922/23.

of Chareau's Surrealist poetry in the Maison de Verre. Our sensory perception is continually perturbed by the incongruity of things – what Rimbaud termed the »derangement of our senses«.

Chareau once wrote: »Only new images excite our emotions!« But the inventive novelties of his – at times baffling, at times magically evocative – installations in the Maison de Verre nevertheless represent a secondary dimension, invoked only once the rational, logical solution underpinning the house had been found. »Architecture is a social art,« said Chareau. »The architect can only create if he listens and understands the voices of millions of men, if he suffers as they do, if he struggles along with them to save them. He employs iron that they have forged, he guides them towards the future because he knows what belongs to the past.«[14]

While it is a fascinating exercise to compare the Maison de Verre with other buildings by Chareau's contemporaries in an effort to ascertain its proper place in the Modern Movement, one is inevitably brought back to the conviction of its utter uniqueness. That Chareau knew the work of Frank Lloyd Wright, for example, through publications and through colleagues such as his own assistant Bernard Bijvoët, is nevertheless indisputable, and the Maison de Verre has more in common with Wright's »textile block« houses in California than one might initially imagine: the pervasive use of a module and grid in

Schranktüren (zugegebenermaßen recht unwahrscheinlich vom praktischen Standpunkt aus gesehen) hätte zur Folge, daß sich die architektonischen Räume von den Schlafzimmern und dem Hauptbadezimmer bis zum Salon und zur Glasbausteinfassade an der Vorderfront des Hauses gegenseitig durchdringen würden.

Des weiteren läßt das Haus Räume innerhalb der Räume erkennen, die durch am Gebäude befestigte bewegliche Elemente geschaffen werden – abermals ein erklärtes Dauerthema in Chareaus Arbeit. Ein konkretes Beispiel hierfür sind die beweglichen Paravents in den beiden Kinderzimmern, die Waschbecken und Bidet vom übrigen Raum abgrenzen. Diese Entwürfe aus Metallrohr und Lochblech – Nachkommen der herkömmlichen Paravents, hinter denen sich die Leute umkleideten – sind auf Rollen vollkommen ausbalanciert und lassen sich ohne Mühe lautlos hin- und herbewegen. Sie verändern auf wirksame Weise den Schlafraum in einer subtilen, ja theatralischen Weise; sie unterteilen den Raum, ohne ihn wirklich zu teilen, weil sie transparent bleiben. Diese Paravents geben eine gedrängte Darstellung der Zusammenarbeit zwischen dem künstlerisch denkenden Chareau und dem genialen Meisterhandwerker Dalbet. Ebenso wie die Bücherregale und die Badewanneneinheit sind die Paravents mehr als bloße Einrichtungsgegenstände und werden Teil der von Chareau geschaffenen surrealistischen Stimmung in der Maison de Verre. Unsere Sinneswahrnehmung wird immer wieder gestört durch die Nicht-Übereinstimmung der Dinge – was Arthur Rimbaud als das »Durcheinanderbringen unserer Sinne« bezeichnete.

Chareau schrieb einmal: »Nur neue Bilder regen unsere Gefühle an!« Doch seine – manchmal verwirrenden, manchmal seltsam evokativen – originellen Neuheiten beim Inventar der Maison de Verre stellen eine untergeordnete Dimension dar, die erst geschaffen wurde, als die rationale, logische Lösung gefunden worden war, die das Haus untermauerte. »Architektur ist eine gesellschaftliche Kunst«, sagte Chareau. »Der Architekt kann nur schaffen, wenn er den Stimmen von Millionen von Menschen zuhört und sie auch versteht, wenn er leidet, wie sie leiden, wenn er mit ihnen zusammen kämpft, um sie zu retten. Er verwendet Eisen, das sie ge-

en Californie qu'on pourrait l'imaginer: emploi de plus en plus répandu du module et d'une trame pour organiser les espaces intérieurs, utilisation d'un unique matériau (le verre dans le cas de Chareau, le bloc de ciment dans celui de Wright) pour la façade intérieure et extérieure, de même que le désir de l'architecte que sa maison serve de modèle à la future demeure populaire. D'autre part, la Maison de Verre pourrait utilement être comparée au travail de certains architectes allemands, notamment les expériences avec les meubles encastrés effectuées sous la direction d'Ernst May, et les types de maisons mis au point par Mies van der Rohe, en commençant par le Pavillon de Barcelone en 1929 et en continuant par les projets des années trente.

On ne peut pas ne pas reconnaître l'influence exercée par l'œuvre de Chareau sur ses propres contemporains, aussi bien dans le domaine du design – comme on le voit dans l'œuvre de René Herbst, Gabriel Guévrékian, Eileen Gray et d'autres encore – que dans le domaine de l'architecture. Le Corbusier, qui fut aperçu à plusieurs reprises par Madame Dalsace alors qu'il était en train de jeter un coup d'œil furtif sur le chantier de la Maison de Verre, commença à employer le même acier et le même verre dans de nombreux projets après 1930 (Cité de Refuge, immeuble Clarté, etc.). Paul Nelson suivit les idées de Chareau dans un projet de maison «suspendue», et par la suite, Eugène Beaudouin et Marcel Lods devaient collaborer avec Jean Prouvé à une école en plein air à Suresnes qui innova non seulement en matière d'acier et de verre, mais aussi en matière de problèmes de chauffage au sol.

L'élévation de la Maison de Verre au rang de quasi-icône dans notre propre génération peut être datée des années soixante, époque à laquelle elle fut «redécouverte» par de jeunes architectes britanniques. La maison, qui fut le sujet d'articles publiés la même année (1966) indépendamment l'un de l'autre par Kenneth Frampton et Richard Rogers, coïncidait avec un regain d'intérêt pour les structures en acier et en verre symbolisées par le bâtiment d'ingénierie de l'université de Leicester réalisé par James Stirling en 1963. L'architecture de Rogers et de Norman Foster, son ancien associé des années soixante, montre une profonde fascination pour les aspects tech-

Vue depuis une fenêtre de la façade côté jardin de la Maison de Verre.

View from window in the garden façade of the Maison de Verre.

Blick aus dem Fenster der Gartenfassade der Maison de Verre.

ordering the interior spaces, the utilisation of a single same material (glass in Chareau's case, cement block in Wright's) for the inner and outer façade, and the architect's intent that the house should serve as a model for future popular housing. On the other hand, the Maison de Verre could be usefully compared with the work of certain German architects, notably the experiments with built-in furniture under the direction of Ernst May, and the housing types developed by Mies van der Rohe, beginning with the Barcelona pavilion in 1929 and continuing in the projects of the 1930s.

The influence of Chareau's work on his own contemporaries was unmistakable, both in the realm of furniture design – as reflected in the work of René Herbst, Gabriel Guévrékian, Eileen Gray and others – and architecture. Le Corbusier, who was spotted by Madame Dalsace on several occasions peeking into the construction site of the Maison de Verre, began to employ the same steel and glass in numerous projects after 1930 (Cité de Réfuge, Clarté, etc.). Paul Nelson pursued Chareau's ideas in a project for a Suspended House, and later Eugène Beaudouin and Marcel Lods were to collaborate with Jean Prouvé on an open-air school in Suresnes which innovated not only with steel and glass, but also with the problems of floor heating.

Elevation of the Maison de Verre to the status of virtual icon in our own generation can be dated to the 1960s, when it was

schmiedet haben, er führt sie in die Zukunft, weil er weiß, was der Vergangenheit angehört.«[14]

Wenn es auch eine faszinierende Übung ist, die Maison de Verre mit anderen Gebäuden von Chareaus Zeitgenossen zu vergleichen in bezug auf den Versuch, ihren richtigen Platz in der Modernen Bewegung zu bestimmen, so gelangt man zwangsläufig zu der Überzeugung, daß sie in höchstem Maße einzigartig ist. Daß Chareau die Arbeiten beispielsweise von Frank Lloyd Wright aus Veröffentlichungen und durch Kollegen, wie seinen eigenen Assistenten Bernard Bijvoët, kannte, ist dennoch nicht zu leugnen. Die Maison de Verre hat mehr gemeinsam mit Wrights »Gewebe-Blockhäusern« in Kalifornien, als man zunächst dachte: die überwiegende Verwendung eines Gittermoduls zur Anordnung der Innenräume, die Verwendung ein und desselben Materials (Glasbausteine bei Chareau, Zementblöcke bei Wright) bei der Innen- und Außenfassade, und die Absicht des Architekten, daß das Haus als Modell für zukünftige Wohnungen dienen sollte. Andererseits könnte die Maison de Verre zweckdienlicherweise mit der Arbeit deutscher Architekten verglichen werden; beachtenswert sind hier u. a. die Experimente mit Einbaumöbeln unter der Leitung von Ernst May und die von Mies van der Rohe entwickelten Wohnungstypen, vom Barcelona-Pavillon im Jahre 1929 bis hin zu den Projekten der dreißiger Jahre.

Unverkennbar beeinflußte Chareaus Werk auch das seiner Zeitgenossen, sowohl im Bereich des Möbeldesigns – wie die Arbeiten von René Herbst, Gabriel Guévrékian, Eileen Gray und anderen zeigen – als auch in der Architektur. Le Corbusier – der, wann immer Frau Dalsace ihn erspähte, einen Blick auf die Baustelle der Maison de Verre werfen mußte – begann bei zahlreichen Projekten nach 1930 (Cité de Réfuge, Clarté etc.) das gleiche Glas und den gleichen Stahl zu verwenden. Paul Nelson verwirklichte Chareaus Ideen in einem Entwurf für ein Hängehaus, und später sollten Eugène Beaudouin und Marcel Lods mit Jean Prouvé an einer Freilichtschule in Suresnes zusammenarbeiten, deren Neuerungen nicht nur in der Verwendung von Glas und Stahl bestanden, sondern auch in der Montage von Fußbodenheizungen.

Die Erhebung der Maison de Verre zum wahren Kultbild in unserer eigenen Gene-

nologiques de la Maison de Verre. La généalogie est complète quand on se souvient que le président du jury qui sélectionna le projet de Piano et de Rogers pour le Centre Pompidou en 1971 n'était autre que Jean Prouvé.

A la mort de Pierre Chareau, son ami de longue date et compagnon designer Francis Jourdain rapporta à la presse une anecdote qui éclaire le côté humoristique et le côté pratique de l'architecte. Jourdain dit qu'il avait eu un jour un rêve dans lequel il regardait monter et descendre un vieil ascenseur français fait de bois et de verre. Il y avait dans l'ascenseur un poêle à bois relié à un tuyau qui s'allongeait et se repliait comme un téléscope à mesure que l'ascenseur montait et descendait. Quand Jourdain se réveilla, le premier nom qui lui vint à l'esprit, comme étant celui de l'inventeur de cette machine, fut celui de Pierre Chareau![15]

L'œuvre de Pierre Chareau, qui est parfois aussi fantastique et charmante qu'elle est révolutionnaire, doit être considérée comme solidement implantée dans le mouvement moderne en Europe pour des raisons clairement exprimées par le philosophe allemand Jürgen Habermas dans son article intitulé «Architecture moderne et post-moderne» (1981).[16] La Maison de Verre illustre la manière dont Habermas voit le mouvement moderne, comme effort inachevé. Chareau, qui a travaillé patiemment et infatigablement pendant des années avec son maître artisan Dalbet, a créé une maison pratique et fonctionnelle qui est une réponse sensible aux besoins et gestes humains particuliers. En même temps, cette maison reflète pourtant une logique intérieure et une liberté artistique frôlant parfois l'obsession, lui donnant une autonomie radicale en tant qu'œuvre d'art et non comme architecture. Elle défie les canons conventionnels de l'architecture et du design. C'est une demeure qui fonctionne intérieurement comme un cadre physique et spatial parfaitement indépendant, pour une personne ayant une activité professionnelle spécifique et sa famille. Elle ne peut être reproduite; personne n'a imité avec succès la Maison de Verre (la rendant «classique» dans un autre sens). Maintenant que la famille d'origine est partie, il est en outre difficile d'y intégrer d'autres fonctions (non domestiques). Plus que toute autre création antérieure ou ultérieure de Chareau, la

»rediscovered« by young British architects. The subject of articles published independently by Kenneth Frampton and Richard Rogers in the same year (1966), the house coincided with the renewed interest in steel and glass structures typified by James Stirling's Leicester University Engineering building of 1963. The architecture both of Rogers and of Norman Foster, his former partner of the 1960s, reveals a profound fascination with technological aspects of the Maison de Verre. The genealogy is complete when one recalls that the president of the jury which selected Piano and Rogers' project for the Pompidou Centre in 1971 was none other than Jean Prouvé.

On the death of Pierre Chareau, his longtime friend and fellow designer Francis Jourdain recounted an anecdote in the press which elucidates both the humorous and the practical side of the architect. Jourdain said that he once had a dream in which he was watching one of the old-fashioned French elevators of wood and glass going up and down. Inside the elevator was a wood-burning stove, with a stovepipe attached which extended and contracted like a telescope as the elevator went up and down. When Jourdain awoke from his dream, the first name that came to his mind as the inventor of such a machine was that of Pierre Chareau![15]

The work of Pierre Chareau, which is at times as fantastic and enchanting as it is revolutionary, must be seen as firmly implanted in the Modern Movement in Europe, and for reasons clearly articulated by German philosopher Jürgen Habermas in his article »Modern and Post-Modern Architecture« (1981).[16] The Maison de Verre exemplifies Habermas' view of modernism as a yet unfinished endeavour. Chareau, working patiently and tirelessly for years together with his master craftsman Dalbet, created a house which is a practical, functional and sensitive response to particular human needs and gestures. At the same time, however, the house reflects an inner logic and artistic licence bordering at times on the obsessional, giving it a radical autonomy as a self-contained work of art, not architecture. It defies the conventional canons of architecture and interior design. It is an abode which functions internally as a perfectly self-contained physical and spatial setting,

ration erfolgte in den sechziger Jahren, als sie von jungen englischen Architekten »wiederentdeckt« wurde. Der Tenor der Artikel, die Kenneth Frampton und Richard Rogers unabhängig voneinander 1966 veröffentlichten, war, daß das Haus mit dem neuerlichen Interesse an Stahl- und Glasbauten übereinstimmte, für das das Gebäude der Technischen Universität in Leicester von James Stirling aus dem Jahre 1963 ein typisches Beispiel war. In der Architektur von Stirlings Partner aus dem Juli 1000, Rogers und Norman Foster, offenbart sich, wie überaus fasziniert sie von den technologischen Aspekten der Maison de Verre waren. Die Genealogie ist vollkommen, wenn man sich ins Gedächtnis ruft, daß der Präsident der Jury, die das Projekt von Piano und Rogers für das Centre Pompidou im Jahre 1971 auswählte, niemand anders war als Jean Prouvé.

Als Pierre Chareau starb, erzählte sein langjähriger Freund und Mitdesigner Francis Jourdain der Presse eine Anekdote, die die humorvolle und die praktische Veranlagung des Architekten erhellte. Jourdain erzählte, daß er einmal einen Traum gehabt habe, in dem er die altmodischen französischen Fahrstühle aus Holz und Glas beim Rauf- und Runterfahren beobachtete. Im Fahrstuhl befand sich ein Ofen mit einem Ofenrohr, das sich wie ein Teleskop verlängerte und verkürzte, wenn der Aufzug hinauf- oder hinunterfuhr. Als Jourdain aus diesem Traum erwachte, fiel ihm als möglicher Erfinder einer solchen Maschine Pierre Chareau ein![15]

Das Werk Pierre Chareaus, das ebenso fantastisch und bezaubernd wie revolutionär ist, muß als tief verwurzelt in der Modernen Bewegung in Europa gesehen werden, und das aus Gründen, die der deutsche Philosoph Jürgen Habermas in seinem Artikel »Moderne und Postmoderne Architektur« (1981) klar und deutlich darlegt.[16] Am Beispiel der Maison de Verre erläutert Habermas seine Sicht des Modernismus als einen noch unvollkommenen Versuch. Chareau, der lange Jahre höchst ausdauernd mit seinem Meisterhandwerker Dalbet zusammenarbeitete, schuf ein Haus, das nicht nur eine praktische und funktionelle, sondern auch eine feinfühlige Antwort auf die besonderen Bedürfnisse und Gebärden des Menschen ist. Zugleich reflektiert das Haus aber auch innere Logik und künstlerische Freiheit – die zeitweise

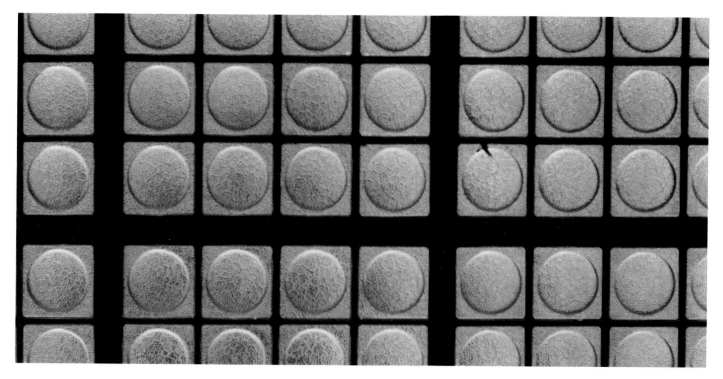

Briques de verre translucides utilisées dans la Maison de Verre.

Translucent glass bricks used in the Maison de Verre.

Durchscheinende Glasbausteine, die beim Bau der Maison de Verre verwandt worden sind.

Maison de Verre est limitée en tant qu'objet, et pourtant presque infiniment riche parce qu'elle suggère toujours d'autres possibilités. Il semble bien que la question par laquelle nous avons commencé – la Maison de Verre est-elle une maison ou un immense meuble? – doive rester sans réponse.

for one specific professional person and his family. It cannot be reproduced; no one has successfully imitated the Maison de Verre (making it »classical« in another sense). When the original family has left, moreover, it may well be difficult to find other (non-domestic) functions to lodge within it. More than any of Chareau's creations before or after, the Maison de Verre is both finite as an object, and yet rich almost without limit in its suggestiveness of still other possibilities. It seems the question with which we began – is the Maison de Verre a house or an immense piece of furniture? – must go unanswered.

an die Grenzen der Besessenheit stoßen –, die ihm eine vollkommene Eigenständigkeit als in sich geschlossenes Kunstwerk und nicht als Bauwerk verleihen. Die Maison de Verre widersetzt sich den konventionellen Grundsätzen von Architektur und Innenarchitektur. Es ist eine Wohnung, die als völlig in sich geschlossenes physisches und räumliches System funktioniert und so die Umgebung für einen bestimmten Menschen mit einem bestimmten Beruf und für seine Familie darstellt. Sie ist nicht reproduzierbar; bislang hat niemand die Maison de Verre erfolgreich nachgebaut (und sie somit in einem anderen Sinn »klassisch« gemacht). Wenn die ursprünglichen Bewohner das Haus einst verlassen haben werden, wird es schwierig sein, andere (nicht auf die Bedürfnisse der Familie abgestimmte) im Haus versteckte Funktionen zu finden. Mehr als jedes andere von Chareaus Werken zuvor oder danach hat die Maison de Verre als Objekt zwar ihre Grenzen, bietet aber in ihren Anregungen und Ideen nahezu unbegrenzte Möglichkeiten. Es scheint also, daß unsere anfängliche Frage – ob die Maison de Verre nun ein Haus oder ein riesiges Möbelstück sei – unbeantwortet bleiben muß.

1 Marc Vellay / Kenneth Frampton, Pierre Chareau, Editions du Regard, Paris 1984
2 Interview de l'auteur en août 1991. / Related in an interview with the author in August, 1991. / Interview mit dem Autor im August 1991.
3 Yve-Alain Bois: «Mondrian en France, sa collaboration à ‹Vouloir›, sa correspondance avec Del Marle», Bulletin de la Soc. Hist. Art français, séance du 7 mars 1981.
4 Adolf Loos: «Architecture», Cahiers d'aujourd'hui, 1913. (Republished in Loos, Paroles dans le Vide, éditions Champ Libre, Paris 1979, p. 219.)
5 Hermann Muthesius: Das englische Haus, 1904. (The English House, London, 1979).
6 Waldemar George: l'Amour de l'Art, n° 3, mars 1923, pp. 483–486.
7 Edmond Fleg: «Nos décorateurs, Pierre Chareau», Les Arts de la Maison, hiver, 1924, p. 17–27.
8 Maurice Raynal / Jacques Lipchitz: Editions Jeanne Bucher, Paris 1947, p. 15.
9 Raymond Cogniat: «L'architecture et l'ameublement au Salon d'Automne» l'Architecture, vol. XLII, #12, 15 dec. 1929, p. 421–456.
10 Jules Henrivaux: La Verrerie au 20e siècle, 1903. Le Palais lumineux de l'exposition Universelle de 1900 était conçu par Latapy, un architecte, et présentait une

gamme vaste de types de verre. / Le Palais lumineux at the 1900 Universal Exhibition was designed by Latapy, an architect, and contained a wide range of types of glass. / Der Palais lumineux auf der Weltausstellung 1900 wurde von dem Architekten Lataby entworfen und wies viele verschiedene Glassorten auf.
11 Glaces et Verres, n° 17, août 1930, p. 19.
12 Bernard Bauchet and Marc Vellay: La Maison de Verre, A.D.A. Edita, Tokyo 1988.
13 Adolf Loos: op. cit., p. 284.
14 «La Maison de Verre», Le Point, II, Colmar, mai 1937, p. 51.
15 E. Besson: «Grand architecte vient de mourir», Ce Soir, sept. 1950.
16 Jürgen Habermas: «Modern and Post-Modern Architecture», 9 H, n° 4, 1982, p. 9–14.

Meubles et intérieurs

Furniture and Interiors

Möbel und Einrichtungen

Bureau et chaises en ébène de Macassar, cabinet du docteur Dalsace, Maison de Verre, vers 1950.

Desk and chairs of macassar ebony in Dr Dalsace's Maison de Verre office, c. 1950.

Tisch und Stühle aus Makassar-Ebenholz in Doktor Dalsaces Büro in der Maison de Verre, um 1950.

Bureau, chaise, tabourets, bibliothèque et lampadaire conçus par Chareau pour le cabinet du docteur Dalsace, 195 Bd Saint-Germain, vers 1920.

Desk, chair, stools, bookcase and floor lamp designed by Chareau for Dr Dalsace's original office at 195 blvd. St. Germain, 1920s.

Tisch, Stuhl, Hocker, Bücherregal und Stehlampe, entworfen von Chareau für das erste Büro von Doktor Dalsace am Boulevard St. Germain Nr. 195; zwanziger Jahre.

1 Lampadaire, vers 1920
1 Floor Lamp, c. 1920
1 Stehlampe, um 1920

2 Chaise (SN38), vers 1919
2 Chair (SN38), c. 1919
2 Stuhl (SN38), um 1919

Intérieur de l'appartement conçu pour Edmond et Madeleine Fleg à Paris; sur la photo datant de la fin des années 20, on voit le buste de E. Fleg réalisé par le sculpteur Chana Orloff.

Interior of the apartment for Edmond and Madeleine Fleg in Paris; photo from the late 1920s, with bust of E. Fleg by Chana Orloff visible.

Wohnungseinrichtung für Edmond und Madeleine Fleg in Paris; Photo aus den späten zwanziger Jahren mit Büste von E. Fleg von Chana Orloff.

Appartement Fleg après son achèvement en 1920, avec estrade et canapé d'angle, table hexagonale et tenture murale sombre.

Fleg apartment soon after completion in 1920, with raised corner couch, hexagonal table, and dark fabric hung from the walls.

Die Flegsche Wohnung bald nach ihrer Fertigstellung im Jahre 1920. Erhöhte Eckcouch, sechseckiger Tisch, Wände mit herabhängendem, dunklem Stoff verkleidet.

3 Guéridon (MB170), vers 1923

3 Pedestal Table (MB170), c. 1923

3 Tisch mit Säulenfuß (MB170), um 1923

Dans cette salle de bains créée par Chareau vers 1920, les murs et une partie du sol sont recouverts de mosaïques en verre.

Bathroom installation by Chareau, c. 1920, includes wall surfaces and part of the floor covered with glass mosaic.

Badezimmereinbau von Chareau, um 1920; Wände und ein Teil des Bodens mit Glasmosaik bedeckt.

La baignoire surélevée se trouve au centre de la pièce avec une douche ouverte appliquée contre le mur.

Raised bathtub is in the centre of the room, with an open shower against the wall.

Erhöhte Badewanne in der Mitte des Raumes, offene Dusche an der Wand.

Etude en couleurs pour la salle de bains réalisée.

Colour study for the executed bathroom.

Farbstudie für das fertige Badezimmer.

Fauteuil gondole de 1922. Son dossier classique, légèrement courbe, a souvent été employé par Chareau, avec de nombreuses variations, y compris des supports courbes ou droits entre les pieds. (MF 11)

Gondola-shaped chair from 1922. Chareau made frequent use of its classical, gently curving back with numerous variations, including curved or straight struts between the legs. (MF 11)

Gondelförmiger Sessel aus dem Jahre 1922. Die klassische, leicht nach hinten gebogene Rückenlehne verwendete Chareau in zahlreichen Abänderungen mit gebogenen oder geraden Verstrebungen zwischen den Beinen. (MF 11)

Fauteuil en bois avec un seul panneau plat au milieu du dossier ou des lattes. La simplicité de sa forme, des matières et de la menuiserie suggère les attaches de Chareau avec les traditions anglaises et continentales, vers 1923. (MF 182)

Wooden armchair with either a single, flat panel in the centre of the back or slats. In its simplicity of shape, materials and joinery, it suggests Chareau's affiliation with English and continental traditions, c. 1923. (MF 182)

Armlehnstuhl aus Holz mit einer einzelnen, flachen Holzplatte oder Leisten in der Mitte der Rückenlehne. Die Einfachheit der Form, der verwendeten Materialien und der Schreinerarbeit zeigt, wie sehr Chareau den britischen und kontinentalen Traditionen verbunden war, um 1923. (MF 182)

Intérieur, vers 1922. On remarquera l'applique, un simple panneau triangulaire en albâtre, et la lampe de table avec un abat-jour fait de panneaux triangulaires en tissu.

Apartment interior, c. 1922. Note the wall lamp, a single, fan-shaped panel of alabaster, and the table lamp with triangular-panelled fabric shade.

Wohnungseinrichtung, um 1922. Bemerkenswert sind die Wandlampe aus einer einzigen, dreieckig geformten Alabasterplatte und die Tischlampe mit dem aus dreieckigen Platten bestehenden Lampenschirm aus Stoff.

4 Bergère (MF15), vers 1920–22

4 Chair »Bergère« (MF15), c. 1920–22

4 Sessel »Bergère« (MF15), um 1920–22

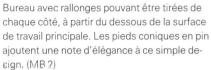

Bureau avec rallonges pouvant être tirées de chaque côté, à partir du dessous de la surface de travail principale. Les pieds coniques en pin ajoutent une note d'élégance à ce simple design. (MB 2)

Writing table with leaves which can be pulled out on either side from beneath the main work surface. The pine-cone feet add a touch of elegance to this simple design. (MB 2)

Schreibtisch mit beidseitig ausziehbaren Seitenbrettern. Die Bretter befinden sich unter der Arbeitsplatte. Die kegelförmigen Füße aus Pinienholz verleihen diesem einfachen Entwurf einen Hauch von Eleganz. (MB 2)

Coiffeuse faite d'une surface plane en quart de cercle et de deux piles de tiroirs placés perpendiculairement l'une par rapport à l'autre; l'ensemble repose sur des pieds ronds ou ovales. 1922–23. (MS 14)

Dressing table comprising a quarter-circle top surface and two stacks of drawers placed perpendicularly to one another; the whole rests on round or oval feet, 1922–23. (MS 14)

Toilettentisch, bestehend aus einer viertelkreisförmigen Tischplatte und zwei rechtwinklig zueinanderstehenden Schubladenelementen. Der Tisch steht auf runden oder ovalen Füßen. 1922–23. (MS 14)

Petite table et chaise (MD 73). La table est le précurseur de diverses coiffeuses avec devant courbe et miroir fixe. La sculpture est de Jacques Lipchitz.

Small table and chair (MD 73). The table is the precursor of numerous dressing tables having a bowed front and mirror attached. Sculpture by Jacques Lipchitz.

Kleiner Tisch und Stuhl (MD 73). Der Tisch ist der Vorläufer verschiedener Toilettentische mit bogenförmiger Vorderseite und fest angebrachtem Spiegel. Skulptur von Jacques Lipchitz.

Chambre de jeune fille dont une étude en couleur (à droite) fut publiée en 1924 (EH 163). Elle contient un lit d'une personne dont les extrémités se courbent autour des côtés; l'ensemble repose sur des pieds sphériques massifs.

Bedroom for a young girl, the study for which was published in colour (right) in 1924 (EH 163). It contains a single bed with headboard and footboard that curve around the sides, the whole resting on solid spherical feet.

Mädchenschlafzimmer, die Studie hierzu (rechts) wurde 1924 in Farbe veröffentlicht (EH 163). Im Raum befindet sich ein Einzelbett auf massiven, kugelförmigen Füßen mit geschwungenem Kopf- und Fußteil.

Etude en couleur pour la chambre.   Colour study for the bedroom.   Farbstudie für das Schlafzimmer.

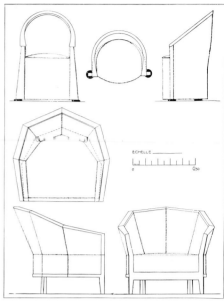

Dessins de chaises exécutés par Chareau, comprenant le modèle MF 172 (1920) et une version de MF 11 (1922).

Drawings of chairs by Chareau including MF 172 (1920) and a version of MF 11 (1922).

Entwürfe für Sessel von Chareau einschließlich MF 172 (1920) und einer Version von MF 11 (1922).

Salon de Madame Hélène Bernheim, vers 1922, dit «Salon Coromandel» et «Salon Chinois» (en haut à gauche et en bas). Décoré avec du bambou et du bois de coromandel pour présenter une collection de panneaux laqués chinois. (ES 66)

The sitting room (above left and below) for Madame Hélène Bernheim, c. 1922. Decorated using bamboo palm and coromandel wood to exhibit a collection of Chinese lacquered panels, it became known as the »Salon de Coromandel« or »Salon Chinois«. (ES 66)

Das für Madame Helene Bernheim um 1922 angefertigte Wohnzimmer (links oben und unten), mit den Spitznamen »Salon de Coromandel« und »Salon Chinois«. Für die Sammlung chinesischer lackierter Tafelbilder wurde der Raum mit Bambuspalmen und Koromandelholz dekoriert. (ES 66)

5　Fauteuil (MF172), vers 1920

5　Armchair (MF172), c. 1920

5　Armsessel (MF172), um 1920

6　Méridienne galbée (MP167), vers 1923

6　Curved Sofa »Méridienne galbée«
　　(MP167), c. 1923

6　Geschwungenes Sofa »Méridienne
　　Galbée« (MP167), um 1923

Reproduction au pochoir en couleur de l'installation du Salon d'Automne (1924).

Colour reproduction in stencil technique of the Salon d'Automne installation (1924).

Farbkopie in Matrizentechnik der Salon-d'Automne-Einrichtung (1924).

Photographie de l'exposition de meubles de Chareau au Salon d'Automne de 1924.

Photograph of Chareau furniture on show at the Salon d'Automne of 1924.

Photographie der Ausstellung von Chareau-Möbeln in der Ausstellung Salon d'Automne im Jahre 1924.

7 Fauteuil (MF220), vers 1922

7 Armchair (MF220), c. 1922

7 Armlehnsessel (MF220), um 1922

8 Fauteuil (MF158), vers 1928
8 Armchair (MF158), c. 1928
8 Sessel (MF158), um 1928

9 Canapé (MP 158), vers 1928
9 Couch (MP 158), c. 1928
9 Couch (MP 158), um 1928

10 Fauteuil (SN37), vers 1923

10 Armchair (SN37), c. 1923

10 Sessel (SN37), um 1923

11 Fauteuil avec dossier régable (MF219),
    vers 1923

11 Armchair with Reclining Back (MF219),
    c. 1923

11 Sessel mit verstellbarer Rückenlehne
    (MF219), um 1923

12 Table basse (MB130), vers 1924
12 Low Table (MB130), c. 1924
12 Niedriger Tisch (MB130), um 1924

13 Table basse (MB106), vers 1924
13 Low Table (MB106), c. 1924
13 Niedriger Tisch (MB106), um 1924

Chambre à coucher, vers 1923.

Bedroom ensemble, c. 1923.

Schlafzimmerensemble, um 1923.

Chambre à coucher de jeune homme, 1923–24. (EH 162)

Bedroom ensemble for a young man, 1923–24. (EH 162)

Schlafzimmerensemble für einen jungen Mann, 1923–24. (EH 162)

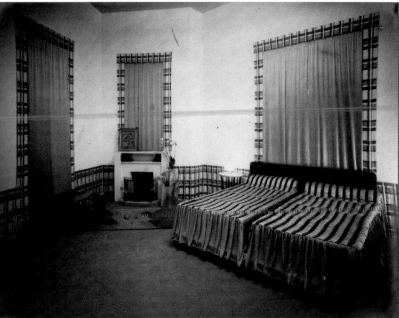

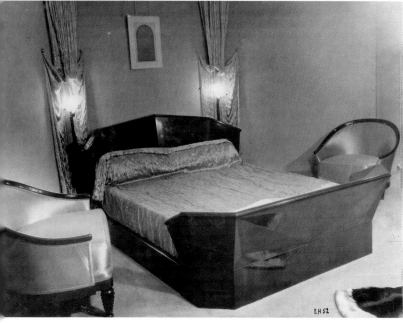

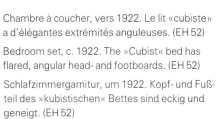

Chambre à coucher, vers 1922. Le lit «cubiste» a d'élégantes extrémités anguleuses. (EH 52)

Bedroom set, c. 1922. The »Cubist« bed has flared, angular head- and footboards. (EH 52)

Schlafzimmergarnitur, um 1922. Kopf- und Fußteil des »kubistischen« Bettes sind eckig und geneigt. (EH 52)

Décoration et meubles de chambre à coucher, vers 1922. On remarquera le guéridon et le couvre-lit fait de peaux, tous deux fréquemment utilisés par Chareau. (EH 145)

Bedroom decoration and furniture, c. 1922. Note the pedestal table and animal-skin bed cover, both frequently used by Chareau. (EH 145)

Schlafzimmerdekoration und Möbel, um 1922. Bemerkenswert sind der Sockeltisch und die Bettdecke aus Fell; beides wurde häufig von Chareau verwendet. (EH 145)

Dessin au pochoir en couleur de la chambre exposée au Salon des Artistes Décorateurs de 1922.

Bedroom ensemble exhibited at the 1922 Salon des Artistes-Décorateurs.

Schlafzimmerensemble in der Aussellung Salon des Artistes Décorateurs von 1922.

14 Table (MB14), vers 1922/23
14 Table (MB14), c. 1922/23
14 Tisch (MB14), um 1922/23

15 Lit d'enfant, 1923
15 Child's Bed, 1923
15 Kinderbett, 1923

Chambre d'enfant, vers 1923. Chareau en conçut beaucoup. Il employa souvent de l'osier pour réaliser les meubles. Le compartiment en filet sous la table de chêne sert à ranger les jouets (exposé au Salon des Artistes Décorateurs en 1923).

Interior of a child's bedroom, c. 1923. He frequently used wicker for furniture. The drawer of netting under the oak table is for storing toys (exhibited at the Salon des Artistes-Décorateurs in 1923).

Eine der vielen von Chareau entworfenen Kinderzimmereinrichtungen; diese entstand um 1923. Er verwendete häufig Flechtwerk für Möbel. Das herausziehbare Netz unter dem Eichentisch dient der Aufbewahrung von Spielzeug (ausgestellt im Salon des Artistes Décorateurs im Jahre 1923).

16 Fauteuil en bois, 1923
16 Wooden Armchair, 1923
16 Armlehnstuhl aus Holz, 1923

17 Chaise, 1923
17 Chair, 1923
17 Stuhl, 1923

18 Table à langer, 1923
18 Nursery Dressing Table, 1923
18 Wickeltisch, 1923

Plafonnier comprenant deux blocs d'albâtre
creux suspendus à une mince plaque de métal.
(LT 314)

Ceiling lamp comprising two hollow blocks of
alabaster suspended from a thin metal plate.
(LT 314)

Deckenlampe aus zwei hohlen Alabasterblök-
ken, aufgehängt an einer dünnen Metallplatte.
(LT 314)

Applique comportant deux blocs d'albâtre
placés côte à côte contre une plaque métallique
et séparés par une surface métallique en forme
de T. (LA 550)

Wall lamp comprising two blocks of alabaster
placed side by side against a metal plate, separated by a T-shaped metal divider. (LA 550)

Wandlampe aus zwei Alabasterblöcken. Die
Blöcke sind Seite an Seite gegen eine Metall-
platte gesetzt und durch ein T-förmiges Stück
Metall voneinander getrennt. (LA 550)

19 Lampe de table, vers 1924

19 Table Lamp, c. 1924

19 Tischlampe, um 1924

20 Lampe de table (LP180), 1922

20 Table Lamp (LP180), 1922

20 Tischlampe (LP180), 1922

Exposition au Salon d'Automne, probablement en 1924, avec lampadaire dit «La Religieuse», en métal et albâtre, conçu par Chareau; chenets et bas-relief de Jacques Lipchitz. (ES 165)

Exhibition at the Salon d'Automne, most probably in 1924, featuring the floor lamp nicknamed »The Nun« in metal and alabaster by Chareau, and irons and bas-relief by Jacques Lipchitz. (ES 165)

Ausstellung im Salon d'Automne, höchstwahrscheinlich im Jahre 1924, mit Stehlampe »Die Nonne«, in Metall und Alabaster von Chareau, und Eisen und Basrelief von Jacques Lipchitz. (ES 165)

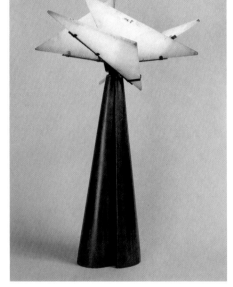

21 Lamp de table, vers 1923

21 Table Lamp, c. 1923

21 Tischlampe, um 1923

Stand d'exposition de meubles de Chareau, publié en 1922. Le bureau a une rallonge coulissante de chaque côté.

Exhibit of furniture by Chareau, published in 1922. The desk has extensions which pull out from either side.

Ausstellungsstand von Chareau-Möbeln, gezeigt im Jahre 1922. Der Tisch besitzt auf beiden Seiten hochklappbare Verlängerungen.

22 Lampadaire (SN31), 1923

22 Floor Lamp (SN31), 1923

22 Stehlampe (SN31), 1923

Chevalet en fer forgé avec éclairage vertical fixe
pour exposer des toiles. (PW 280)

Wrought-iron easel with attached overhead
light fixture for exhibiting paintings. (PW 280)

Staffelei aus Schmiedeeisen mit montierter
Leuchte, die Gemälde wirkungsvoll zur Geltung
bringt. (PW 280)

▽ Etude en couleur montrant l'éclairage indirect
mobile sur rails, vers 1924.

Colour study showing mobile indirect lighting
on rails, c. 1924.

Farbstudie, die die bewegliche indirekte Beleuchtung auf Schienen zeigt, um 1924.

◁ Etagères en plaques de fer forgé suspendues à une rainure métallique fixée au plafond. Leur hauteur est réglable, et l'ensemble peut être déplacé le long de la rainure selon diverses positions. (PD 698)

Bookshelves of wrought-iron plates suspended from an iron rail at ceiling level. The height of the shelves can be adjusted, and the whole assemblage may be moved to different positions along the rail. (PD 698)

Bücherregale aus Schmiedeeisenplatten. Die Platten hängen an Eisenschienen, die an der Decke befestigt sind. Die Regale sind höhenverstellbar und können entlang der Schiene in verschiedene Positionen gebracht werden. (PD 698)

△
Ici, la rampe d'éclairage et les supports pour les étagères sont fixés, mais les étagères peuvent être ajustées. La jardinière métallique est également de Chareau et Dalbet, la sculpture est de Jacques Lipchitz, vers 1924.

Both the ramp of lights and the shelf brackets are here fixed in place, while the shelves can be adjusted. The metal plant holder is also by Chareau and Dalbet. Sculpture by Jacques Lipchitz, c. 1924.

Hier sind die Beleuchtungsrampe und die Halter für die Regale fest angebracht, die Regale können jedoch verstellt werden. Der Pflanzenhalter aus Metall ist ebenfalls von Chareau und Dalbet. Skulptur von Jacques Lipchitz, um 1924.

23 Applique, vers 1923
23 Wall Lamp, c. 1923
23 Wandlampe, um 1923

Sofa-canapé ovale (MP 169) et chaise-gondole (MF 172) recouverts de motifs géométriques, et lampes en albâtre et en métal inspirées du cubisme. Chareau se servait fréquemment de rideaux mi-longs ou longs pour recouvrir les murs, 1923–24. (EL 302)

Oval-shaped sofa (MP 169) and »gondola« chair (MF 172) upholstered in geometric patterns, and alabaster and metal lights inspired by Cubism. Half-length or full-length curtains were often used by Chareau to cover walls, 1923/24. (EL 302)

Ovales Sofa (MP 169) und »Gondel«-Sessel (MF 172) mit geometrischen Mustern, und Beleuchtung aus Metall und Alabaster, inspiriert vom Kubismus. Als Wandverkleidung benutzte Chareau häufig halblange oder lange Vorhänge, 1923–24. (EL 302)

Le fauteuil à dossier haut et droit (MF 1002) de cet appartement redécoré, 1925–27, contraste avec le fauteuil au dossier inclinable.

The tall straight-backed chair (MF 1002) in this redecorated apartment, 1925–27, contrasts with the easy chair whose back can be inclined to different positions.

Der hohe Sessel mit gerader Rückenlehne (MF 1002) in dieser neudekorierten Wohnung, 1925–27, bildet einen Gegensatz zu dem Sessel mit der verstellbaren Rückenlehne.

24 Fauteuil à dossier haut (MF1002),
1924–27

24 High-backed Armchair (MF1002),
1924–27

24 Sessel mit hoher Rückenlehne (MF1002),
1924–27

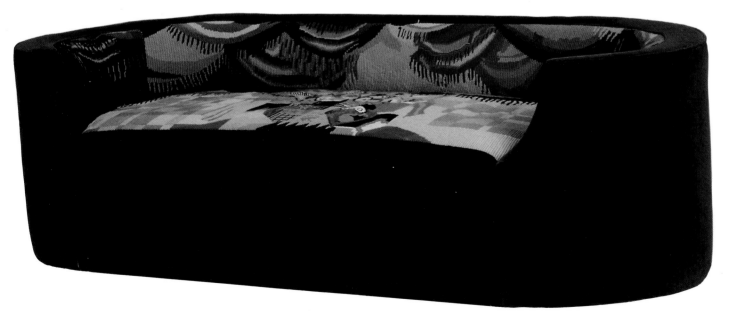

25 Sofa-canapé (MP169), 1923

25 Couch (Sofa canapé) (MP169), 1923

25 Couch (Sofa Kanapee) (MP169), 1923

26 Tabouret (MT1015), vers 1923
26 Stool (MT1015), c. 1923
26 Hocker (MT1015), um 1923

Installation de Chareau à l'Exposition des Arts Décoratifs au Pavillon de Marsan, en 1927. Le bureau (SN 6) conçu en 1926 est en palissandre et fer forgé. On remarquera en outre les panneaux pliants en éventail fixés au plafond, qui glissent le long d'une rainure au sol.

Installation by Chareau at the Exposition d'art décoratif in the Pavilion Marsan, 1927. Desk (SN 6) designed in 1926 is a combination of rosewood and wrought iron. Note also the fan-like folding panels attached to the ceiling, which slide along a groove in the floor.

Einrichtung von Chareau in der Ausstellung Exposition d'art décoratif im Pavillon Marsan, 1927. In dem 1926 entworfenen Tisch (SN 6) wurde Palisander mit Schmiedeeisen kombiniert. Bemerkenswert sind außerdem die an der Decke befestigten, fächerähnlich aufklappbaren Paneelen, die entlang einer Rille im Boden gleiten.

Dessin d'un appartement meublé par Chareau, vers 1926.

Drawing of an apartment furnished by Chareau, c. 1926.

Entwurf einer von Chareau ausgestatteten Wohnung, um 1926.

27 Sofa-canapé (MP287), 1924

27 Couch (MP287), 1924

27 Couch (MP287), 1924

Intérieur et meubles conçus pour le Pavillon de l'Indochine à l'Exposition Internationale des Arts Décoratifs de Paris, en 1925. Le buffet et le placard furent spécialement fabriqués pour cette exposition.

Interior and individual pieces of furniture conceived for the Indochina Pavilion at the 1925 Exposition International des Arts Décoratifs et Industriels Modernes in Paris. Sideboard and cupboard were made especially for the exhibit.

Einrichtung und einzelne Möbelstücke, entworfen für den Indochina-Pavillon auf der Internationalen Ausstellung dekorativer Künste in Paris im Jahre 1925. Anrichte und Schrank wurden in erster Linie als Ausstellungsstücke angefertigt.

Dessin pour le pavillon de l'Indochine, 1925.   Drawing of the Indochina Pavilion, 1925.   Zeichnung für den Indochina Pavillon, 1925.

Détail du bureau-bibliothèque conçu par Chareau pour une ambassade de France et exposé à l'Exposition Internationale des Arts Décoratifs à Paris en 1925. Les panneaux coulissants en éventail peuvent être ouverts pour protéger et dissimuler les étagères et les casiers quand on ne s'en sert pas.

Detail of Chareau's office and library for a French Embassy exhibited at the 1925 Exposition Internationale des Arts Décoratifs et Industriels Modernes in Paris. The fan-like sliding panels can be opened in order to protect and conceal the shelves and cabinets when not in use.

Detail aus Chareaus Büro und Bibliothek für eine französische Botschaft, ausgestellt auf der Internationalen Ausstellung der dekorativen Künste in Paris im Jahre 1925. Die Schiebepaneelen lassen sich fächerähnlich aufklappen, um die Regale und Büroschränke abzuschirmen und sie zu verbergen, wenn sie nicht benötigt werden.

Dessin du même bureau-bibliothèque, y compris le bureau et le fauteuil de l'ambassadeur. On aperçoit également des panneaux de bois en éventail servant à voiler la lumière reflétée par la coupole située au-dessus de l'espace central.

Drawing of the same office-library, including the ambassador's desk and chair. Also depicted are suspended wooden fan-like panels used to obscure the reflected light from the cupola over the central space.

Entwurf derselben Büro-Bibliothek, einschließlich Schreibtisch und Stuhl des Botschafters. Ebenfalls dargestellt sind fächerähnliche, hängende Holzpaneelen, die dazu dienen, das von der Kuppel über der Mitte des Raumes einfallende Licht abzuschwächen.

28 Bureau (MB212), 1925

28 Desk (MB212), 1925

28 Schreibtisch (MB212), 1925

29 Table de jeux pliante (MB241), vers 1929
29 Folding Games Table (MB241), c. 1929
29 Zusammenklappbarer Spieltisch
     (MB241), um 1929

30 Bureau (MB1055), vers 1926
30 Writing Table (MB1055), c. 1926
30 Schreibtisch (MB1055), um 1926

31 Coiffeuse (MS1009), 1926/27
31 Dressing Table (MS1009), 1926/27
31 Toilettentisch (MS1009), 1926/27

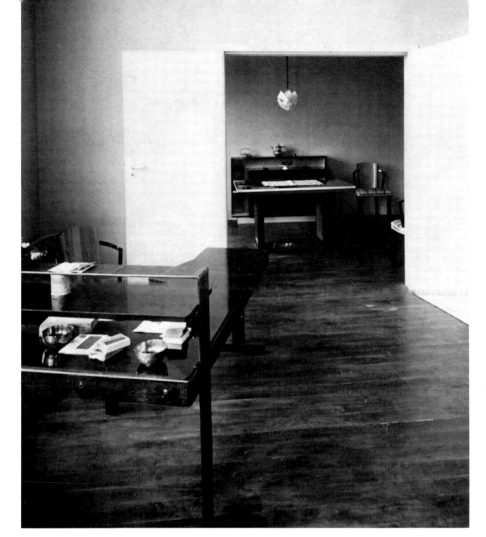

Bureau en palissandre et fer forgé (MB 405). Il existe de nombreuses variantes de ce bureau, y compris un modèle pour l'architecte français Robert Mallet-Stevens.

Desk of rosewood and wrought iron (MB 405). Numerous variations of this desk exist, including one for French architect Robert Mallet-Stevens.

Tisch aus Palisander und Schmiedeeisen (MB 405). Von diesem Tisch existieren zahlreiche Varianten, darunter auch die für den französischen Architekten Robert Mallet-Stevens.

Intérieur de l'appartement de Pierre Chareau, où les idées, telles que les supports pour peintures et meubles, étaient développées au début, vers 1927. Peintures de Braque, de Juan Gris, de Picasso et d'autres encore, et sculpture de J. Lipchitz. (EB 408)

The interior of Pierre Chareau's own apartment, where ideas such as the supports for paintings and pieces of furniture were initially developed, c. 1927. Paintings by Braque, Juan Gris, Picasso and others, as well as sculpture by Lipchitz. (EB 408)

Die Einrichtung von Pierre Chareaus eigener Wohnung, in der die Ideen, wie z. B. die Halter für Gemälde und Möbelstücke, zuerst entwickelt wurden (um 1927). Gemälde von Braque, Juan Gris, Picasso und anderen; Skulptur von J. Lipchitz. (EB 408)

32 Bureau (MB673), vers 1927
32 Desk (MB673), c. 1927
32 Schreibtisch (MB673), um 1927

33 Tabouret (SN3), vers 1927
33 Stool (SN3), c. 1927
33 Hocker (SN3), um 1927

34 Ensemble coiffeuse et tabouret (MS423
   & MT1015), vers 1926/27

34 Dressing Table and Stool Ensemble
   (MS423 & MT1015), c. 1926/27

34 Toilettentisch und Hocker, Ensemble,
   (MS423 & MT1015), um 1926/27

Exposition de meubles de Chareau à la Galerie
Barbazanges à Paris, en 1926. L'équilibre de la
coiffeuse et du miroir reposant sur trois pieds
en fer forgé, fixés avec des charnières, dépend
de l'angle selon lequel ils sont placés. On remarquera la peinture de Giorgio de Chirico choi-
sie par Chareau. (EZ 435)

Exhibition of Chareau furniture at the Galerie
Barbazanges in Paris, 1926. The dressing table
and mirror resting on three wrought-iron legs,
attached with hinges, depend upon the angle at
which they are placed to maintain their equilibrium. Note the painting by Giorgio de Chirico
selected for inclusion by Chareau. (EZ 435)

Ausstellung von Chareau-Möbeln in der Galerie
Barbazanges in Paris, 1926. Der Toilettentisch
und der Spiegel sind durch Gelenke miteinander verbunden und stehen auf drei schmiedeeisernen Beinen. Die beiden Elemente halten ihr
Gleichgewicht, indem man sie in einem bestimmten Winkel zueinander aufstellt. Bemerkenswert ist das Gemälde von Giorgio de Chirico, das von Chareau ausgewählt und in die
Ausstellung miteinbezogen wurde. (EZ 435)

35 Coiffeuse avec meuble pour cosmétiques (MS418), vers 1927

35 Dressing Table with Cosmetic Cabinet
   (MS418), c. 1927

35 Toilettentisch mit Kosmetikschrank
   (MS418), um 1927

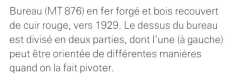

Bureau (MT 876) en fer forgé et bois recouvert de cuir rouge, vers 1929. Le dessus du bureau est divisé en deux parties, dont l'une (à gauche) peut être orientée de différentes manières quand on la fait pivoter.

Office desk (MT 876) of wrought iron and wood covered with red leather, c. 1929. The top is divided into two parts, of which one (here, left) can be pivoted to different angles.

Bürotisch (MT 876) aus Schmiedeeisen und mit rotem Leder überzogenem Holz, um 1929. Die Tischplatte besteht aus zwei voneinander getrennten Platten, wovon eine (nach links) durch Schwenken in verschiedene Winkel eingestellt werden kann.

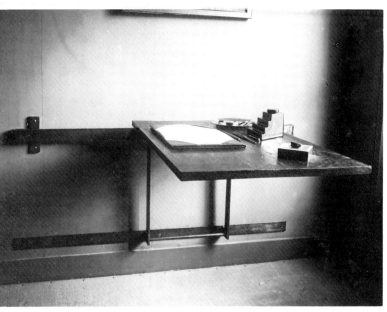

Console en fer forgé et bois, attachée à des rails horizontaux fixés au mur; elle peut être déplacée le long d'un axe. (MB 410)

This wall table of wrought iron and wood, attached to horizontal rails fixed to the wall, may be moved to different positions along a single axis. (MB 410)

Wandtisch aus Schmiedeeisen und Holz. Der Tisch ist an horizontalen, an der Wand befestigten Schienen angebracht und läßt sich entlang einer einzelnen Achse in verschiedene Positionen bringen. (MB 410)

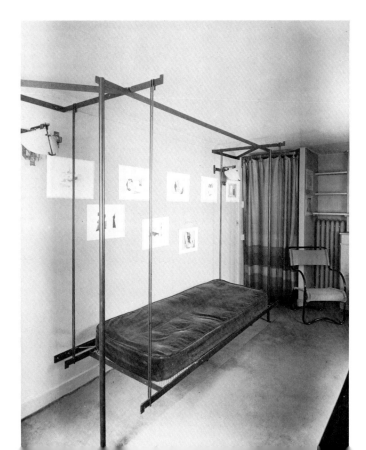

Lit-balançoire suspendu à un cadre en fer forgé, 1927. Présenté à l'Exposition des Arts Décoratifs de Paris en 1925; un exemplaire fut installé ultérieurement sur la terrasse de la villa conçue par Mallet-Stevens pour le Vicomte de Noailles à Hyères.

Swing bed suspended from a wrought-iron frame, 1927. Shown at the 1925 Exposition Internationale des Arts Décoratifs in Paris, a version was later installed on the roof-terrace of the villa designed for the Vicomte de Noailles at Hyères by Mallet-Stevens.

Das Schaukelbett hängt an einem Rahmen aus Schmiedeeisen, 1927. Ausgestellt im Jahre 1925 auf der Ausstellung Dekorative Kunst in Paris. Ein Modell wurde später auf der Dachterrasse der Villa eingebaut, die Mallet-Stevens für den Grafen de Noailles in Hyères entworfen hatte.

36 Table de bureau (MT876), vers 1929

36 Office Table (MT876), c. 1929

36 Bürotisch (MT876), um 1929

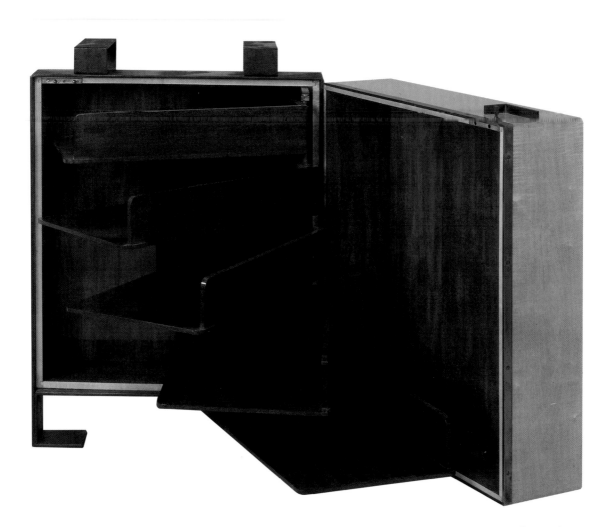

37 Coffre à linge (MA373), vers 1927
37 Linen Chest (MA373), c. 1927
37 Wäschetruhe (MA373), um 1927

38 Armoire, vers 1923
38 Armoire, c. 1923
38 Schrank, um 1923

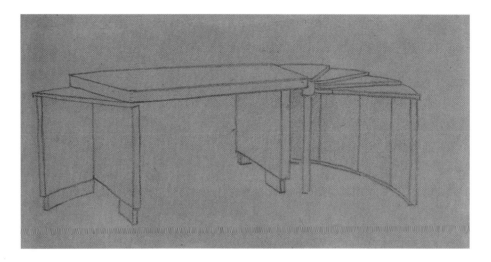

Dessin préparatoire de P. Chareau. Bureau réalisé en acajou de Cuba, vers 1928. Dessus de table rectangulaire fixe et surfaces de travail triangulaires pivotant vers l'extérieur de chaque côté : une série de quatre tables sur la droite, une seule table sur la gauche.

Preparatory drawing by Chareau, and the finished desk/table in Cuban mahogany, c. 1928. A fixed, rectangular table-top ends in triangular work surfaces which pivot outwards on either side: a nest of four tables on the right, and a single table to the left.

Vorentwurf von Chareau. Der fertige Schreibtisch/Tisch aus kubanischem Mahagoni, um 1000. Eine unveränderliche, rechteckige Tischplatte und eine dreieckige Arbeitsfläche, die sich auf beiden Seiten nach außen drehen lassen: rechts ein Satz von vier Tischen, links ein einzelner Tisch.

39   Table basse (MB152), vers 1925
39   Low Table (MB152), c. 1925
39   Niedriger Tisch (MB152), um 1925

Fumoir-salle de jeux et bar du Grand Hôtel de Tours redécoré par Chareau en 1928. Les meubles comportent des chaises cubistes (MF 313) recouvertes de cuir vert, des tabourets en acajou et en métal, et des guéridons. Des écrans métalliques courbes, maintenus en place par des rails en bas et en haut et des bras métalliques partant d'un point central situé au plafond (repr. p. 88), peuvent être fermés pour séparer les deux espaces. Une mosaïque en acajou est appliquée sur certains murs. (HT 583)

Smoking/games room and bar in the Grand Hotel at Tours redecorated by Chareau in 1928. Furniture includes Cubist chairs (MF 313) covered in green leather, stools of mahogany and metal, and pedestal tables. Curved solid metal screens, held in place by a rail below and metal arms from a focal point on the ceiling (see ill. p. 88), can be closed in order to separate the two spaces. Mahogany mosaic is applied on some walls. (HT 583)

Raucher-/Spielzimmer und Bar im Grand Hotel in Tours, von Chareau neu dekoriert im Jahre 1928. Unter den Möbeln befinden sich kubistische Sessel, die mit grünem Leder bezogen sind (MF 313), Hocker aus Mahagoni und Metall, und Tische mit Untergestell. Um die beiden Räume voneinander zu trennen, können die bogenförmig verlaufenden Zwischenwände aus Metall geschlossen werden. Unten gleiten die Wände auf einer Schiene; oben werden sie von fächerförmig angeordneten Metallarmen gehalten (siehe Abb. S. 88). An einigen Wänden wurde ein Mahagonimosaik angebracht. (HT 583)

40 Fauteuil club (MF313), vers 1926
40 Fireside Chair (MF313), c. 1926
40 Kaminsessel (MF313), um 1926

41 Chaise (MF276), vers 1924
41 Chair (MF276), c. 1924
41 Stuhl (MF276), um 1924

42 Tabourets de bar (MT344), 1926
42 Bar Stools (MT344), 1926
42 Barhocker (MT344), 1926

Grand Hôtel de Tours (voir repr. p. 87 en haut)
Grand Hotel at Tours (see ill. p. 87 above)
Grand Hotel in Tours (siehe Abb. S. 87 oben)

43 Table de jeux, vers 1928

43 Games Table, c. 1928

43 Spieltisch, um 1928

Table circulaire basse fixée par une charnière à une bibliothèque courbe en sycomore ou en poirier, et reposant sur une sphère métallique.

Low, circular table attached by a hinge to a curved bookcase of sycamore or pear-tree wood, resting on a single metal sphere to allow for movement.

Niedriger, runder Tisch, der mit einem Gelenk an einem gerundeten Bücherregal aus Sykomore oder Birnbaumholz befestigt ist. Damit der Tisch beweglich ist, steht er auf einer einzigen Metallkugel.

Table de salle à manger. Les quatre pieds en fer forgé reposant chacun sur une sphère métallique permettent de déplacer facilement la table, vers 1930. (EM 980)

Dining-room table. The four wrought-iron legs each hold a metal sphere, permitting the table to be moved easily, c. 1930. (EM 980)

Eßzimmertisch. Die vier schmiedeeisernen Beine halten je eine Metallkugel, so daß der Tisch leicht verschoben werden kann, um 1930. (EM 980)

44 Table, vers 1927

44 Table, c. 1927

44 Tisch, um 1927

Chaise métallique pliante (voir repr. p. 93).

Folding metal chair (see ill. p. 93).

Zusammenklappbare Metallstühle (siehe Abb. S. 93).

Le pavillon du club de golf de Beauvallon, France, fut conçu en 1926 par Chareau en collaboration avec l'architecte hollandais Bernard Bijvoët pour Emile Bernheim, oncle d'Annie Dalsace.

The golf Clubhouse in Beauvallon, France, was conceived by Chareau in collaboration with Dutch architect Bernard Bijvoët in 1926, for the uncle of Anna Dalsace, Emile Bernheim.

Das Golfklubhaus in Beauvallon, Frankreich, entwarf Chareau in Zusammenarbeit mit dem holländischen Architekten Bernard Bijvoët im Jahre 1926 für den Onkel von Annie Dalsace, Emile Bernheim.

La collection de meubles conçue pour le pavillon du club illustre la richesse des formes et des matières employées.

The collection of furniture designed for the Clubhouse displays a rich variety of forms and materials.

Die für das Klubhaus entworfene Möbelkollektion veranschaulicht die bunte Vielfalt der verwendeten Formen und Materialien.

45 Chaise (MC767), vers 1927

45 Chair (MC767), c. 1927

45 Stuhl (MC767), um 1927

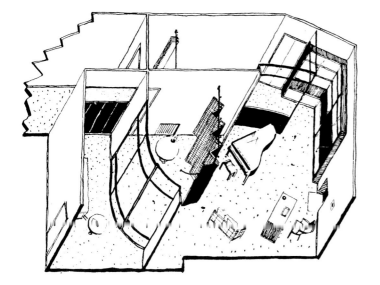

Axonométrie de l'agencement de l'appartement de la famille Farhi à Paris en 1930/31.

Axonometric drawing of the 1930/31 apartment
installation for the Farhi family in Paris.

Axonometrischer Entwurf der Wohnungseinrichtung für die Familie Fahri in Paris im Jahre
1930/31.

◁ ▽ ▷ ▷

Les espaces intérieurs peuvent être isolés ou
ouverts à l'aide de cloisons pliantes ou coulissantes en bois, en métal et en verre. Quand
l'écran est rabattu, les coins séjour et repas for-
ment un seul espace.

The interior spaces can be isolated or opened
up by means of folding or sliding partitions of
wood, metal and glass. With the screen folded
back, the living and dining areas become one
space.

Durch Falt- oder Schiebewände aus Holz, Glas
oder Metall lassen sich die Innenräume voneinander trennen oder miteinander verbinden.
Durch Zurückfalten der Faltwände werden
Wohn- und Eßbereich zu einem Raum.

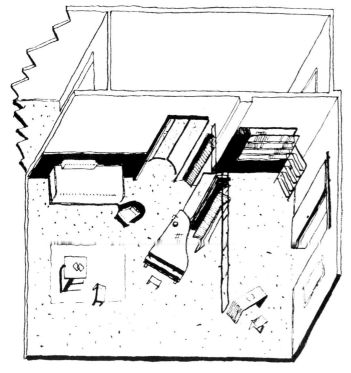

Axonométrie d'une partie de l'appartement de Daniel Dreyfus à Paris, vers 1931. Deux salons sont séparés par un écran pliant en palissandre et cuir rouge suspendu à un cadre métallique.

Axonometric drawing of part of the Daniel Dreyfus apartment in Paris, c. 1931. Two salons are separated by a folding screen of rosewood and red leather hung from a metal frame.

Axonometrischer Entwurf eines Teils der Wohnung von Daniel Dreyfus in Paris. Zwei Salons werden durch eine Faltwand aus Palisander und rotem Leder getrennt, die Faltwand an einem Metallrahmen hängt.

◁ ▽ ▷ ▷

Les pièces de l'appartement Dreyfus peuvent être séparées par un écran en bois et en cuir rouge. La bibliothèque en fer forgé et en palissandre (gauche) comprend deux éléments verticaux, l'un plus bas que l'autre, reliés par une charnière, de sorte que la position de l'élément inférieur peut être ajustée. Le salon principal est séparé du hall d'entrée par une porte coulissante courbe en verre supendue au plafond.

The rooms in the Dreyfus apartment can be separated by a wood and red leather screen. The wrought-iron and rosewood bookcase (left) has two upright elements, one lower than the other, hinged together so that the position of the lower element may be adjusted. The main salon is separated from the entry hall by a curved, glazed sliding door suspended from the ceiling.

Die einzelnen Zimmer in der Wohnung der Dreyfus' können durch eine Faltwand aus Holz und rotem Leder geteilt werden. Der Bücherschrank aus Schmiedeeisen und Palisander (links) verfügt über zwei unterschiedlich hohe, gerade Elemente, die durch Gelenke miteinander verbunden sind. Eine gewölbte verglaste Schiebetür, die an der Decke hängt, trennt den Hauptraum von der Eingangshalle.

46 Table basse en tubes et en verre,
    vers 1932

46 Low Tubular and Glass Table, c. 1932

46 Niedriger Rohr- und Glastisch, um 1932

Salle de bains (maintenant démolie) et meubles de Chareau dans une villa qui existe toujours près de Genève, vers 1928. La douche se trouve derrière une cloison en verre armé convexe.

Bathroom installation (now demolished) and furniture by Chareau for an existing villa near Geneva, c. 1928. The shower is located behind a curved, reinforced glass partition.

Badezimmerinstallation (nun herausgerissen) und Möbel von Chareau für eine noch bestehende Villa in der Nähe von Genf, um 1928. Die Dusche befindet sich hinter einer gewölbten, verstärkten Trennwand aus Glas.

Dans la même villa, Chareau conçut et meubla une chambre pour deux enfants, vers 1928. Il ne reste que les bureaux sur lesquels les enfants faisaient leurs devoirs: une tablette en bois, dissimulé sous chaque fenêtre, pivote dans la pièce quand on s'en sert.

In the same villa, Chareau designed and furnished a bedroom for two children, c. 1928. All that remains are the children's desks: wooden tabletops, concealed beneath each window, which pivot into the room when in use.

In derselben Villa entwarf und möblierte Chareau ein Schlafzimmer für zwei Kinder, um 1928. Die einzigen noch verbliebenen Möbelstücke sind die Schreibtische der Kinder: unter den Fenstern verborgene Tischplatten aus Holz, die sich zum Arbeiten in den Raum drehen läßt.

Chaises en tubes d'acier présentées au Salon des Arts Ménagers à Paris en 1937. Commanditées par l'OTUA et construites par la Compagnie Parisienne d'Ameublement. (SN 34) Les tables (non montrées) pouvaient être démontées, les chaises commodément empilées dans un potit espace.

Tubular steel chairs, exhibited at the 1937 Salon des Arts Ménagers in Paris. Sponsored by the OTUA and constructed by the Compagnie Parisienne d'Ameublement. (SN 34) The tables (not shown) could be disassembled and the chairs conveniently stacked in a small volume of space.

Stahlrohrstühle, die 1937 im Salon des Arts Ménagers in Paris ausgestellt wurden. Gesponsert von der OTUA und gebaut von der Compagnie Parisienne d'Ameublement. (SN34) Die Tische (nicht abgebildet) konnten auseinandergenommen und die Stühle entsprechend platzsparend ineinandergestapelt werden.

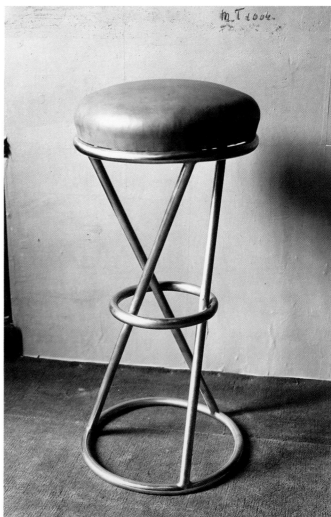

Tabouret en forme de bobine composé de trois anneaux en tubes métalliques reliés par des pieds posés en oblique. Le siège est en cuir, vers 1930. (MT 1004)

Stool in the shape of a bobbin, composed of three tubular metal rings, joined by legs set at oblique angles. The seat is of leather, c. 1930. (MT 1004)

Spulenförmiger Hocker, bestehend aus drei Ringen aus Metallrohr, die durch schiefwinklige Beine miteinander verbunden sind. Der Sitz ist aus Leder, um 1930. (MT 1004)

Intérieur des bureaux de LTT rénovés par Chareau en 1932

Interior of the LTT offices renovated by Chareau in 1932.

Inneneinrichtung der von Chareau im Jahre 1932 renovierten LTT Büroräume.

Vues de la maison de Djémil Anik, 1927
Views of the Djémil Anik house, 1927.
Ansichten des Hauses für Djémil Anik, 1927.

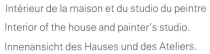

Intérieur de la maison et du studio du peintre
Interior of the house and painter's studio.
Innenansicht des Hauses und des Ateliers.

Extérieur de la hutte préfabriquée convertie en maison de week-end et studio par Pierre Chareau pour le peintre Robert Motherwell, 1948

Exterior of the weekend house and studio in a Quonset hut, converted by Pierre Chareau for the painter Robert Motherwell, 1948

Außenansicht des Wochenendhauses und der Studios in einer umgebauten Militärbaracke für den Maler Robert Motherwell, 1948.

La Maison de Verre

The House of Glass

Das Haus aus Glas

Maquette de la Maison de Verre, faite par Dindeleux, exposée au Salon d'Automne de 1931.

Model of the Maison de Verre, made by Dindeleux, exhibited at the 1931 Salon d'Automne.

Modell der Maison de Verre von Dindeleux, das auf dem 1931er Salon d'Automne ausgestellt wurde.

◁

La nuit, quand elle est éclairée de l'intérieur, la Maison de Verre luit comme une lanterne chinoise, ou un immense écran translucide au travers duquel les ombres se déplacent comme dans un jeu d'ombres.

At night, when lit only from the interior, the Maison de Verre glows like a Chinese lantern, or a huge translucent screen, across which shadows move as in a shadow play.

Nachts, wenn das Haus nur von innen beleuchtet wird, leuchtet die Maison de Verre wie ein chinesischer Lampion oder wie eine gewaltige lichtdurchlässige, beleuchtete Wand, über die die Schatten huschen wie in einem Schattenspiel.

Maison de Verre
Plan du rez-de-chaussée et du jardin

1. Passage d'entrée
2. Cour de devant
3. Garage pour deux voitures
4. Bâtiment XVIIIe siècle existant
5. Entrée de la maison (rez-de-chaussée)
6. Entrée de la maison (étages supérieurs)
7. Aile de service
8. Entrée du jardin
9. Terrasse du bureau du docteur
10. Lierre
11. Pelouse et arbustes
12. Dallage

Maison de Verre
Plan of the ground floor and garden

1. Entrance passageway
2. Front courtyard
3. Garage for two cars
4. Existing eighteenth-century building
5. Entrance to house (ground floor)
6. Entrance to house (upper floors)
7. Service wing
8. Entrance to garden
9. Terrace of the doctor's office
10. Ivy
11. Grass and shrubs
12. Paving stones

Maison de Verre
Grundriß von Erdgeschoss und Garten

1. Zufahrt
2. Vorderer Hof
3. Garage mit zwei Stellplätzen
4. Bestehendes Gebäude
   aus dem 18. Jahrhundert
5. Eingang zum Haus (Erdgeschoß)
6. Eingang zum Haus (obere Etagen)
7. Trakt mit Nutzräumen
8. Eingang zum Garten
9. Zum Sprechzimmer des Doktors gehörende
   Terrasse
10. Efeu
11. Rasen und Sträucher
12. Pflasterstein

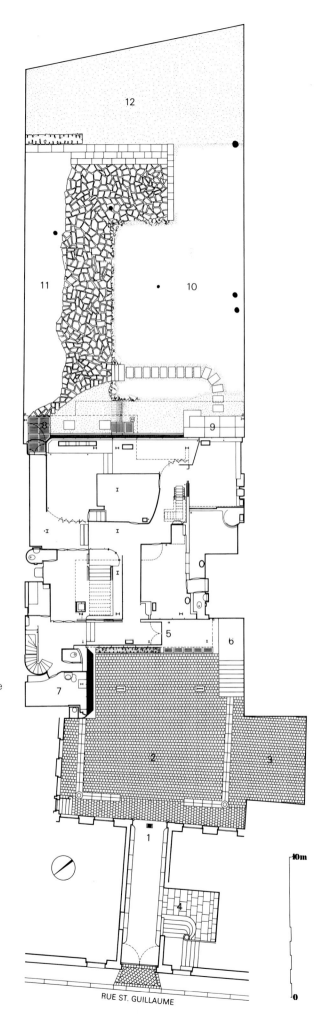

RUE ST. GUILLAUME

a

b

a Le petit hôtel particulier XVIIIe siècle situé au centre de Paris que les Dalsace voulaient raser afin de construire une maison moderne.

The original 18th-century townhouse in Paris, which the Dalsaces had intended to demolish completely in order to build a modern house.

Das im Geschäftsviertel von Paris gelegene Original-Stadthaus aus dem 18. Jahrhundert. Die Dalsaces wollten das Haus vollständig abreißen, um dann ein modernes Haus zu bauen.

b La vieille maison fut sauvée par un locataire qui refusa de quitter l'étage supérieur. Une structure métallique fut donc introduite sous cet étage et seule la partie inférieure fut démolie.

Prevented from totally demolishing the old house by a tenant who refused to vacate the top floor, a metal structure was inserted beneath this floor and only the lower part was demolished.

Der vollständige Abriß des alten Hauses wurde von einem Mieter verhindert, der das obere Stockwerk nicht räumen wollte. Unter dieses Stockwerk wurde daher eine Metallkonstruktion gesetzt, während der untere Teil des Hauses abgerissen wurde.

c

c Les architectes employèrent des dalles de verre translucides mesurant 20 × 20 × 4 cm pour réaliser la façade principale donnant sur la cour et celle de l'aile cuisine/buanderie de la nouvelle maison, vers 1929.

Translucent glass bricks, measuring 20 cm × 20 cm × 4 cm, were employed for the main courtyard façade and that of the kitchen/utility wing of the new house, c. 1929.

Für die Haupthof-Fassade des neuen Hauses und die der Küche/des Traktes, in dem sich die Nutzräume befinden, verwendeten die Architekten lichtdurchlässige Glasbausteine mit den Maßen 20 cm × 20 cm × 4 cm.

d La façade donnant sur le jardin, où se trouvent le cabinet du docteur, un petit salon et les chambres, est composée de dalles de verre, de verre transparent et de panneaux métalliques, vers 1929.

The opposite, garden façade, behind which the doctor's offices, a small sitting room and bedrooms are located, is composed of glass bricks, transparent glass and metal panels, c. 1929.

Die gegenüberliegende Gartenfassade, wo sich die Praxisräume des Doktors, ein kleines Wohnzimmer und Schlafräume befinden, besteht aus Glasbausteinen, durchsichtigem Glas und Metallplatten, um 1929.

d

Un détail de la façade principale au crépuscule montre à la fois la lumière réfléchie et la lumière venant de l'intérieur.

A detail of the main façade at twilight shows reflected light as well as light from inside.

Die Detailaufnahme der Hauptfassade in der Dämmerung zeigt nicht nur reflektiertes Licht, sondern auch das Licht aus dem Inneren des Hauses.

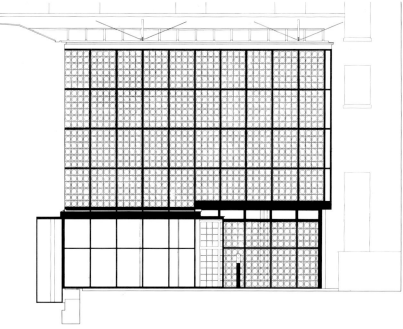

Dessin de la façade principale.
Drawing of the main façade.
Zeichnung der Hauptfassade.

La façade côté jardin conserve son apparence et son harmonie d'origine.

The garden façade retains its original appearance and harmony when compared to the front.

Im Vergleich zur Vorderseite behält die Gartenfassade ihr ursprüngliches Aussehen und ihre harmonische Struktur bei.

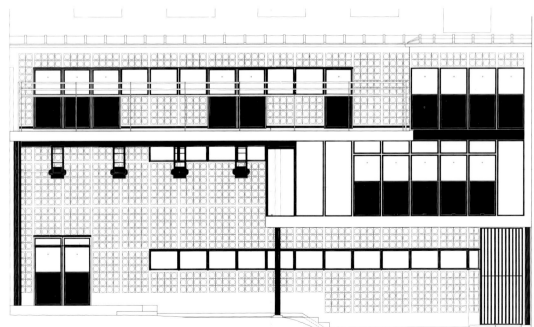

Dessin de la façade côté jardin.
Drawing of the garden façade.
Zeichnung der Gartenfassade.

Plan du rez-de-chaussée

1. Entrée
2. Couloir principal
3. Couloir menant au jardin
4. Salle d'attente
5. Réception
6. Cabinet de consultation du docteur
7. Salle d'examens
8. Chirurgie
9. Vestiaire
10. Escalier latéral menant au bureau
11. Escalier principal menant au salon
12. Pièce réservée aux domestiques
13. Entrée des fournisseurs
14. Monte-plats
15. Ascenseur
16. Escalier menant au sous-sol
17. Escalier menant à la cuisine
18. Poubelles

Plan of the ground floor

1. Entrance
2. Main corridor
3. Corridor leading to garden
4. Waiting room
5. Reception
6. Doctor's consulting room
7. Examination room
8. Surgery
9. Cloakroom
10. Side staircase to the study
11. Main staircase to living room
12. Servants' quarters
13. Tradesmen's entrance
14. Dumbwaiter
15. Elevator
16. Staircase to basement
17. Staircase to kitchen
18. Garbage bins

Grundriß des Erdgeschosses

1. Eingang
2. Hauptkorridor
3. Korridor zum Garten
4. Wartezimmer
5. Rezeption
6. Sprechzimmer des Doktors
7. Untersuchungsraum
8. Operationssaal
9. Garderobenraum
10. Nebentreppe zum Arbeitszimmer
11. Haupttreppe zum Wohnzimmer
12. Dienstbotenunterkünfte
13. Lieferanteneingang
14. Speisenaufzug
15. Aufzug
16. Kellertreppe
17. Treppe zur Küche
18. Mülltonnen

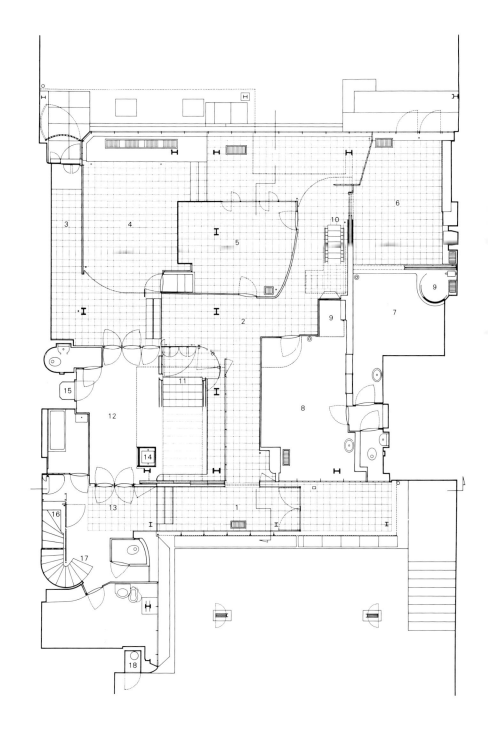

Baigné d'une douce lumière indirecte côté jardin, le cabinet du docteur est un espace sur deux étages, la seule pièce donnant directement sur le jardin.

Bathed in soft indirect natural light on the garden side, the doctor's office is a double-height space, the only room with direct access to the garden.

Das auf der Gartenseite in weiches, indirektes natürliches Licht getauchte Sprechzimmer des Doktors ist doppelt so hoch wie die anderen Räume. Es ist auch der einzige Raum, mit direktem Zugang zum Garten.

La réception a des panneaux de verre encadrés par du métal; ils pivotent et s'ouvrent. Quand les fenêtres donnant sur le jardin sont aussi ouvertes, la ventilation est excellente. Visuellement, Chareau aime multiplier le nombre d'appareils faisant écran et au travers desquels on peut voir.

The receptionist's office has metal-framed glass panels which pivot open; with the windows onto the garden also open, there is excellent cross-ventilation. Visually, Chareau likes to multiply the number of transparent screening devices.

Das Büro der Sprechstundenhilfe hat metallgerahmte, schwenkbare Glasbaustein-Platten; wenn die Fenster zum Garten hin ebenfalls geöffnet sind, ist der Raum ausgezeichnet belüftet. Chareau neigte dazu, die Zahl der transparenten Trennwände rein optisch zu erhöhen.

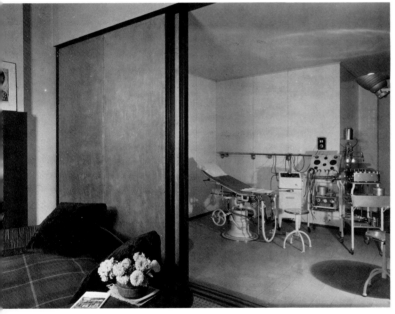

Salle d'examens adjacente au cabinet du docteur.

An examination room adjacent to the doctor's office.

Ein Untersuchungsraum grenzt unmittelbar an das Sprechzimmer des Doktors.

A partir de l'entrée du cabinet du docteur, un escalier spécial, seulement fixé en haut et en bas, permet d'accéder facilement à son bureau privé.

From the entrance to the doctor's office, a special staircase, fixed only at the top and bottom, allows easy access to his private study.

Vom Eingang zum Sprechzimmer aus ermöglicht eine ungewöhnliche Treppe, die nur oben und unten befestigt ist, den Zugang zum privaten Arbeitszimmer des Doktors.

Une rangée de fenêtres le long du couloir menant au cabinet du docteur offre une vue sur le
jardin. Les fenêtres peuvent être ouvertes sé-
parément ou simultanément. Des gaines de
chauffage placées sous les sols amènent l'air
chaud vers des orifices, juste sous les fenêtres.

A row of windows along the corridor to the doctor's office offers a view onto the garden. Windows can be opened separately, or simultaneously as one. Heating pipes under the floors
bring hot air to outlets just below the windows.

Eine Fensterreihe entlang des Korridors, der
zum Sprechzimmer des Doktors führt, bietet
Aussicht auf den Garten. Die Fenster lassen
sich sowohl einzeln als auch gleichzeitig, wie
ein einziges Fenster, öffnen. Heizungsrohre unter dem Boden bringen heiße Luft zu Abzug-
söffnungen, die sich unmittelbar unter den Fenstern befinden.

Deux portes, l'une courbe et l'autre droite, séparent les pièces familiales du cabinet du docteur situé au rez-de-chaussée. Toutes deux sont faites de verre transparent et d'écrans métalliques perforés qui peuvent régler la quantité de lumière naturelle pénétrant dans le couloir. Chareau a qualifié l'escalier principal menant du cabinet médical à l'appartement d'«échelle monumentale».

Two doors, one curved and the other straight, separate the family rooms from the doctor's ground floor offices. Both are composed of transparent glass and perforated metal screens which can control the amount of natural light entering the corridor. The main stairs from the offices to the apartment were referred to by Chareau as a »monumental ladder«.

Zwei Türen, eine gewölbt, die andere gerade, trennen die Familienräume von den Praxisräumen im Erdgeschoß. Beide Türen bestehen aus transparentem Glas und Trennwänden aus Lochblech, so daß der Einfall des natürlichen Lichts in den Korridor reguliert werden kann. Die Haupttreppe, die von den Praxisräumen zur Wohnung führt, bezeichnete Chareau als »monumentale Leiter«.

L'escalier, qui semble flotter sur un vide parce qu'il n'y a ni contremarches ni rampe, est orienté vers la façade principale en briques de verre; le visiteur qui le monte pour accéder au salon peut apprécier les effets dramatiques de la lumière et des matières.

The stairs are oriented towards the main glass brick façade; without risers and handrails, they seem to float over a void. Visitors ascending to the salon are thereby exposed to the full dramatic impact of the light and the material.

Die Treppe, die über einem leeren Raum zu schweben scheint, weil sie weder Futterstufen noch Handlauf besitzt, ist zur Hauptglasbausteinfassade hin ausgerichtet; ein Besucher, der die Treppe zum Salon hinaufgeht, kommt so in den Genuß der überwältigenden Effekte, die das Licht und das verwendete Material hervorrufen.

Plan du premier étage

1. Palier
2. Salon principal
3. Salle à manger
4. Petite pièce d'irradiation
5. Bureau
6. Vide de la salle d'attente
7. Vide du cabinet de consultation
8. Projecteurs
9. Serre
10. Escalier mobile menant à la chambre princi-
    pale
11. Cabine téléphonique
12. Escalier menant au cabinet de consultation
13. Etagères basses
14. Escalier menant à la cuisine
15. Entrée de la cuisine
16. Cuisine
17. Garde-manger
18. Monte-plats
19. Escalier menant au deuxième étage
20. Ascenseur
21. Placard à balais pivotant
22. Rangement
23. Rangement
24. Passe-plats

Plan of the first floor

1. Landing
2. Main living room
3. Dining room
4. Small sun room
5. Study
6. Area above waiting room
7. Area above consulting room
8. Flood lights
9. Conservatory
10. Retractable ladder to main bedroom
11. Telephone booth
12. Staircase down to consulting room
13. Low bookshelf units
14. Staircase to kitchen
15. Entrance to kitchen
16. Kitchen
17. Pantry
18. Dumbwaiter
19. Staircase to second floor
20. Elevator
21. Revolving broom closet
22. Storage units
23. Storage room
24. »Passe-plat« pivoting shelf

Grundriß der ersten Etage

1. Treppenabsatz
2. Hauptwohnzimmer
3. Speisezimmer
4. Kleiner Sonnenraum
5. Arbeitszimmer
6. Bereich über dem Wartezimmer
7. Bereich über dem Sprechzimmer
8. Scheinwerfer
9. Wintergarten
10. Einziehbare Leiter zum großen Schlafzim-
    mer

11. Telefonzelle
12. Zum Sprechzimmer hinunterführende
    Treppe
13. Niedrige Bücherregalelemente
14. Treppe zur Küche
15. Eingang zur Küche
16. Küche
17. Anrichteraum
18. Speiseaufzug
19. Treppe zum zweiten Stockwerk
20. Aufzug
21. Drehbarer Besenschrank
22. Möbelelemente zur Verwendung als
    Stauraum
23. Vorratskammer
24. »Passe-plat« schwenkbares Regalbrett

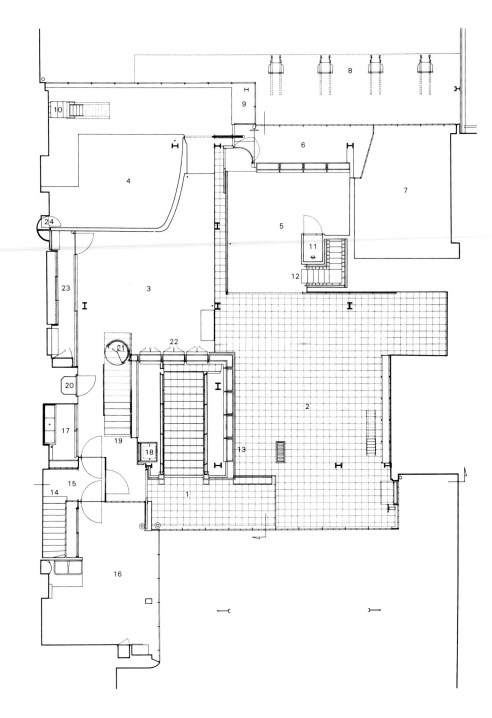

Vue du palier à travers la maison vers le jardin.
Le salon se trouve à droite, le bureau privé du
docteur au-delà, et le coin salle à manger à
gauche.

View from the landing through the house towards the garden. The salon is to the right, with
the doctor's private study beyond, and the dining area to the left.

Blick vom Treppenabsatz durch das Haus zum
Garten. Salon auf der rechten Seite, weiter hinten das private Arbeitszimmer des Doktors, Eßbereich auf der linken Seite.

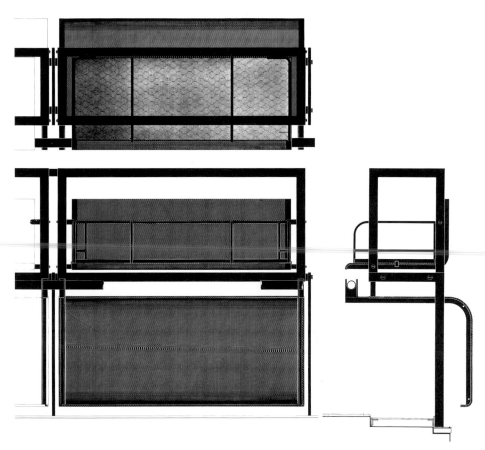

Dessin de l'élément bibliothèque qui forme une balustrade autour de l'escalier principal et est combiné avec des meubles de rangement au second étage.

Drawing of the bookshelf element which forms a balustrade around the main stairs, and is combined with cabinets on the second floor.

Entwurf für das Bücherregal-Element, das eine Ballustrade rund um die Haupttreppe bildet. Das Element ist zudem mit den Schränken im zweiten Stockwerk verbunden.

Le cadre en fer forgé des rayons à livres fait un angle de 90° et devient le cadre des placards à linge dans la salle à manger. On remarquera sur la photo le plateau suspendu à des rails au plafond, plateau qui servait à transporter les plats de la cuisine à la salle à manger.

The wrought-iron frame of bookshelves makes a 90-degree turn and becomes the frame for linen cabinets in the dining room. Note the tray suspended from rails on the ceiling, which was used to carry dishes from the kitchen to the dining room.

Der schmiedeeiserne Rahmen der Bücherregale bildet einen 90-Grad-Winkel und wird dann zum Rahmen für die Wäscheschränke im Wohnzimmer. Bemerkenswert auf dem Photo ist das von Schienen an der Decke hängende Tablett, das benutzt wurde, um das Geschirr aus der Küche ins Eßzimmer zu bringen.

Un placard à balais cylindrique en métal est situé dans l'espace repas, sous l'escalier menant au second étage. Le module carré des briques de verre et des carreaux en caoutchouc est répété dans l'écran métallique entre l'escalier et le couloir.

A cylindrical metal broom closet is located in the dining area, beneath the stairs to the second floor. The square module of the glass bricks and the rubber floor tiles is here repeated in the steel-wire screen between the stairs and hallway.

Im Eßbereich befindet sich unter der Treppe, die zum zweiten Stockwerk führt, ein zylinderförmiger Besenschrank aus Metall. Das quadratische Modul der Glasbausteine und des Bodenbelags aus Gummi wiederholt sich hier in der Zwischenwand aus Stahldraht zwischen Treppe und Korridor.

La salle de séjour principale avec les portes coulissantes fermées donnant sur le bureau privé du docteur et la zone de repos.

The main living room with the sliding doors to the doctor's private study and rest area closed.

Der Hauptwohnraum; die Schiebetüren zu dem privaten Arbeits- und Ruheraum des Arztes sind geschlossen.

◁

Le principal espace collectif de la maison est cette salle de séjour sur deux étages, utilisée également pour les activités familiales, les concerts et les réceptions.

◁

The main collective space in the house is this double-height living room, used equally for family activities and for concerts and receptions.

◁

Der Hauptgemeinschaftsraum des Hauses ist dieses doppelstöckige Wohnzimmer. Der Raum wurde gleichermaßen für Familienaktivitäten wie für Konzerte und Empfänge genutzt.

La vue de la salle à manger vers la salle de séjour montre combien les espaces intérieurs de la maison sont étroitement liés, continus et pourtant délimités.

The view from the dining room towards the living room illustrates how interior spaces of the house are interconnected, continuous yet demarcated.

Der Blick vom Eßzimmer auf das Wohnzimmer veranschaulicht, wie die Innenräume des Hauses miteinander verbunden sind: Sie sind zwar zusammenhängend, aber dennoch voneinander abgegrenzt.

▷

Comme on pouvait s'y attendre, l'amour qu'éprouvait Chareau pour le théâtre se révèle dans son chef-d'œuvre architectural. Vue sous cet aspect et éclairée par les projecteurs situés à l'extérieur de la façade de verre, la salle de séjour devient un séjour pour artistes. De plus, le piano qu'utilisait Madame Dalsace pour donner des récitals était alternativement placé sous la mezzanine ou à côté de la façade en dalles de verre.

▷

Not surprisingly, Chareau's love of theatre is revealed in his architectural masterpiece. The living room, seen from this angle and lit by the spotlights outside the glass façade, becomes a space for performers. The piano used by Mme. Dalsace for recitals was alternatively placed beneath the mezzanine or next to the glass brick façade.

▷

Es überrascht nicht weiter, daß sich Chareaus Liebe zum Theater auch in seinem architektonischen Meisterwerk offenbart. Von diesem Standpunkt aus gesehen, wird das Wohnzimmer, dessen Glasfassade außen von Scheinwerfern beleuchtet wird, zu einem Raum für Darsteller. Darüber hinaus wurde der Flügel für Frau Dalsaces Konzertabende entweder unter das Mezzanin oder neben die Glasbaustein-Fassade gestellt.

Détail de la salle à manger.

A detail of the dining room.

Detail des Eßzimmers.

Vue du couloir vers le bureau privé du docteur
et la zone de repos.

View from the corridor to the doctor's private
study and rest area.

Blick vom Flur aus in den privaten Arbeits- und
Ruheraum des Arztes.

Le bureau privé du docteur et espace de repos au premier étage, qui peut être isolé des pièces réservées à la famille à l'aide de portes coulissantes, mais reste toujours à portée de voix et de vue de son cabinet, au-dessous. Un placard proche du lit-banquette fut converti en cabine téléphonique insonorisée peu après l'installation de la famille dans la maison.

The doctor's private study and rest area on the first floor, which can be isolated from the rest of the family quarters by means of sliding doors yet still remain within sight and sound of his offices below. A closet next to the day-bed was converted into a soundproof telephone booth soon after the family occupied the house.

Der private Arbeits- und Ruheraum des Doktors im ersten Stockwerk kann von den anderen Familienräumen durch Schiebetüren abgetrennt werden, bleibt aber dennoch im Hör- und Sichtbereich der Praxisräume im Erdgeschoß. Ein Schrank neben der Bettcouch wurde zu einer schalldichten Telefonzelle umgeformt, kurz nachdem die Familie das Haus bezogen hatte.

L'unité balustrade-bibliothèque en fer forgé, plaques métalliques perforées et verre que l'on trouve dans la salle de séjour est également utilisée dans le bureau du docteur; en outre, le bureau en palissandre et en métal est en harmonie avec la bibliothèque encastrée.

The same bookshelf-balustrade unit of wrought iron, perforated sheet metal and glass found in the living room is also used in the doctor's study. The rosewood and metal desk is aesthetically harmonious with this built-in library »equipment«.

Die gleiche Bücherregal-Ballustrade aus Schmiedeeisen, Lochblech und Glas aus dem Wohnzimmer wurde auch im Arbeitszimmer des Doktors verwendet; zudem harmoniert der Schreibtisch aus Palisander und Metall ästhetisch mit dieser eingebauten Bibliotheks»ausstattung«.

◁ △

Un petit salon, que Chareau appelait quelque-fois «boudoir», était destiné aux réceptions in-times de Madame Dalsace. Le lit-banquette, dont la tête se trouvait contre le mur, était à l'origine muni de roulettes. Le salon servait peut-être aussi de chambre d'amis. Des car-reaux noirs recouvrent le sol comme dans le bureau du docteur.

A small sitting room, sometimes referred to as the »boudoir« by Chareau, was conceived as an intimate reception space for Mme. Dalsace. The day-bed, with head against the wall, origin-ally had rollers on its legs for mobility. It was perhaps intended also as a guest room. Black tiles cover the floor here as in the doctor's study.

Ein kleines Wohnzimmer, das Chareau manch-mal als das »Boudoir« bezeichnete, wurde als persönlicher Empfangsraum für Frau Dalsace entworfen. Die mit dem Kopfende an der Wand stehende Bettcouch hatte ursprünglich Rollen unter den Beinen, damit sie verschoben wer-den konnte. Möglicherweise war der Raum auch als Gästezimmer gedacht. Hier, wie auch im Arbeitszimmer des Doktors, bedecken schwarze Fliesen den Boden.

La chambre principale comprend un lit-banquette métallique sur des roulettes à côté de l'échelle escamotable, ainsi que des meubles dessinés par Chareau, tels que le lit et la commode encastré dans le mur, que les Dalsace amenèrent de leur ancien appartement (voir également repr. p. 135 en bas).

The master bedroom includes a metal day-bed on rollers next to the retractable ladder, as well as furniture designed by Chareau which the Dalsaces brought from their previous apartment, such as the bed and chest of drawers fitted into the wall (see also ill. p. 135 below).

Im Hauptschlafzimmer befindet sich neben der einziehbaren Leiter eine Bettcouch aus Metall, die auf Rollen steht. Außerdem befinden sich viele Möbelstücke im Raum, die Chareau bereits für die frühere Wohnung der Dalsaces entworfen hatte, so zum Beispiel das Bett und die in die Wand eingebaute Kommode (siehe auch Abb. S. 135 unten).

Vue de l'échelle escamotable en position abaissée depuis la chambre principale. La grille, qui est cachée sous le lit-banquette dans cette position, glisse vers l'extérieur sur le vide de l'escalier quand l'échelle est relevée; la barrière de sécurité glisse simultanément le long de rails; les deux éléments servent à empêcher l'utilisateur imprudent de tomber dans l'appareil escamotable.

View from the master bedroom of the retractable ladder in the down position. The grille, which is concealed beneath the day-bed in this position, slides outwards over the void of the stairway as the ladder is brought up; the guard rail also slides simultaneously along a track. Both elements serve to protect the unwary user from falling onto the retractable device.

Blick vom Hauptschlafzimmer auf die heruntergelassene einziehbare Leiter. Das Türgitter, das in dieser Position unter der Bettcouch verborgen ist, schiebt sich beim Hochbringen der Leiter über den leeren Raum der Treppe. Gleichzeitig schiebt sich auch der Handlauf entlang einer Schiene. Beide Elemente dienen dazu, den unvorsichtigen Benutzer der Treppe vor dem Sturz auf die einziehbare Vorrichtung zu bewahren.

Plan du second étage

1. Espace salon
2. Chambre principale
3. Chambre
4. Salle de bains principale
5. Terrasse
6. Couloir-galerie
7. Salle de bains des invités
8. Lingerie
9. Chambre du personnel
10. Projecteurs
11. Monte-plats
12. Ascenseur
13. Placard mural
14. Placard à balais
15. Etagères basses
16. Rangement
17. Penderies
18. Douche
19. Dressing avec équipements de toilette
20. W.C.

Plan of the second floor

1. Area of living room
2. Main bedroom
3. Bedroom
4. Main bathroom
5. Terrace
6. Corridor-gallery
7. Guest bathroom
8. Linen room
9. Staff bedroom
10. Flood lights
11. Dumbwaiter
12. Elevator
13. Wall cupboard
14. Broom cupboard
15. Low bookshelves
16. Storage units
17. Wardrobes
18. Shower
19. Dressing rooms with washing facilities
20. W.C.

Grundriß der zweiten Etage

1. Wohnzimmerbereich
2. Großes Schlafzimmer
3. Schlafzimmer
4. Hauptbadezimmer
5. Terrasse
6. Korridor-Galerie
7. Gästebadezimmer
8. Wäscheraum
9. Personalschlafraum
10. Scheinwerfer
11. Speisenaufzug
12. Aufzug
13. Wandschrank
14. Besenschrank
15. Niedrige Bücherregale
16. Möbelelemente zur Verwendung
    als Stauraum
17. Kleiderschränke
18. Dusche
19. Ankleidezimmer mit Waschgelegenheit
20. Toilette

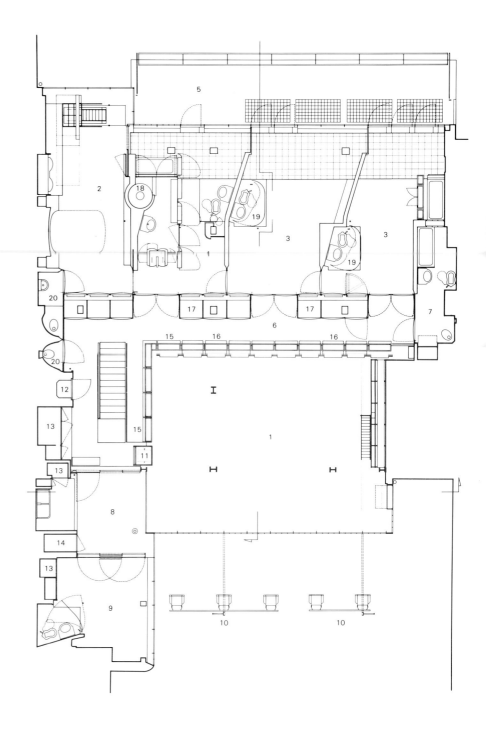

Le couloir du second étage est partiellement caché à la salle de séjour (en bas à droite) par des rayons à livres, des placards et des écrans métalliques pliés et perforés. Du bas, on peut entendre les bruits dans le couloir et peut-être voir des ombres, mais l'intimité est préservée.

The corridor on the second floor is partially concealed from the living room (at right below) by bookshelves, cabinets and folded, perforated metal screens. From below, one can hear movement along the corridor and perhaps see shadows, but privacy is maintained.

Der Korridor im zweiten Stockwerk ist vom Wohnzimmer aus (rechts unten) teilweise verdeckt durch Bücherregale, Schränke und Falttrennwände aus Lochblech. Von unten kann man zwar Schritte entlang des Korridors hören und vielleicht auch Schatten sehen, doch bleibt die Privatsphäre erhalten.

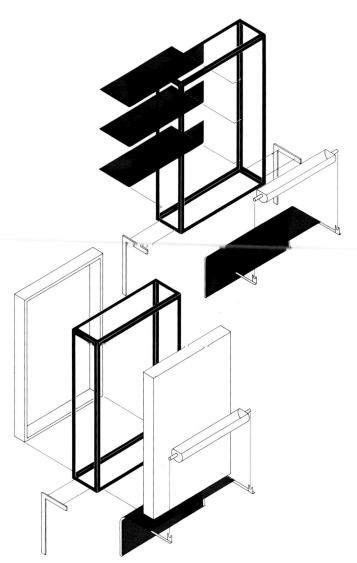

Dessin illustrant les cadres métalliques et les composantes pour rayons à livres et meubles au second étage, avec appareils d'éclairage électrique situés du côté salle à manger de ces unités.

Drawing illustrating the metal frames and the components for bookcases and cabinets on the second floor, with electric light fixtures located on the living-room side of these units.

Die Zeichnung veranschaulicht die Metallrahmen und Bauelemente für Bücherregale und Schränke im zweiten Stockwerk; die auf der Wohnzimmerseite der Elemente angebrachten Lampen sind ebenfalls zu sehen.

Une photographie du hall entre la cuisine et la salle à manger au premier étage montre un rail au plafond, la long duquel un plateau suspendu transportait les plats. On voit également un garde-manger avec cabine de contrôle où aboutissaient les circuits électriques.

A photograph of the hall between the kitchen and the dining room on the first floor reveals a ceiling rail along which a suspended tray carried food and dishes. Also visible is a pantry-cum-junction box where electrical circuits terminated.

Ein Photo, das im Flur zwischen Küche und Eßzimmer im ersten Stockwerk aufgenommen wurde, zeigt die Deckenschiene, an der entlang ein herabhängendes Tablett Speisen und Geschirr beförderte. Ebenfalls zu sehen ist ein Anrichteraum mit Schaltpult, wo elektrisch betriebene Einrichtungen ein- und ausgeschaltet werden können.

D'un point avantageux surplombant la salle de séjour principale, on voit une continuité ou une «transparence» dans l'organisation spatiale de la Maison de Verre. Au travers des portes ouvertes de la salle de bains principale, les façades de verre sont visibles du côté du jardin de même que du côté de la cour principale.

From a vantage point overlooking the main living room one perceives a continuity or »transparency« in the spatial organisation of the Maison de Verre. Through the open doors of the master bathroom, the glass façades of both the garden and the main courtyard are visible.

Von diesem Punkt aus läßt sich der Hauptwohnraum gut überblicken, und man spürt eine gewisse Kontinuität oder »Transparenz« in der räumlichen Gestaltung der Maison de Verre. Durch die geöffneten Türen des Hauptbadezimmers sind die Glasfassade auf der Gartenseite und die Fassade des Haupthofs zu sehen.

La douche et la baignoire sont situées très près l'une de l'autre; toutefois, deux écrans de métal perforé peuvent être ajustés pour fournir un certain degré d'intimité.

The shower and bathtub are located close to one another. Two screens of perforated sheet metal can be adjusted to provide a certain degree of privacy as desired.

Dusche und Badewanne befinden sich dicht beieinander; nach Bedarf können jedoch zwei Trennwände aus Lochblech so gestellt werden, daß eine gewisse Ungestörtheit erreicht wird.

La douche et l'espace toilette sont séparés du lavabo et du bidet par de minces placards en duralumin. La porte de l'un d'eux (que l'on voit partiellement ouverte) s'adapte avec précision contre la cloison en face (sur la gauche) quand elle est complètement ouverte; elle divise effectivement l'espace temporairement et augmente l'intimité . . . dans une salle de bains comportant CINQ entrées.

Shower and dressing areas are secluded from the wash basin and bidet by shallow cabinets of duraluminium. The door of one of these (seen here partially open) fits precisely against the partition opposite it (on the left) when it is fully opened; it thereby effectively divides the space temporarily and increases privacy – in a bathroom that has *five* entrances.

Dusche und Ankleidebereich sind von Waschbecken und Bidet durch flache Duraluminiumschränke abgetrennt. Die Tür eines dieser Schränke (hier teilweise geöffnet zu sehen) paßt genau gegen den gegenüberliegenden Raumteiler (links), wenn sie ganz geöffnet ist. Auf diese Weise wird der Raum zeitweilig effektvoll geteilt und das Maß an Ungestörtheit erhöht – in einem Badezimmer mit fünf Eingängen.

Les placards en duralumin glissent le long d'une rainure, tournent et la porte s'ouvre en pivotant pour montrer une pile de tiroirs qui pivotent également en tant qu'unité, et les tiroirs peuvent être sortis. Cinq mouvements en tout.

The duraluminium chests conceal a total of five movements: they can be slid along a rail and pivoted open; their doors pivot open in turn to reveal a stack of drawers which also pivot as a unit; and these drawers then pull out.

Die Duraluminiumkommoden gleiten entlang einer Schiene und lassen sich auseinanderdrehen; die Tür läßt sich durch Drehen nach hinten öffnen, und zum Vorschein kommen übereinanderliegende Schubfächer, die ebenfalls als Einheit drehbar sind, die Schubfächer können herausgezogen werden. Insgesamt also fünf Bewegungen.

Les cintres métalliques pour vêtements de la salle de bains principale sont fixés en permanence à la tringle tubulaire, bien qu'ils soient fixés sur une glissière.

The chests of drawers in the master bathroom sit on a duraluminium pedestal, seen here as one enters from the main corridor.

Die Kommoden im Hauptbadezimmer stehen auf einem Sockel aus Duraluminium. Blick auf die Kommoden beim Betreten des Badezimmers vom Hauptflur aus.

Le bloc de placards mobils de la salle de bains principale se trouve sur des pieds en duralumin, on le voit ici quand on entre en venant du couloir principal.

The metal clotheshangers in the master bathroom are permanently fixed to the tubular rod, although they can be slid along the groove into which they are set.

Die Kleiderhaken aus Metall im Hauptbadezimmer sind fest an der röhrenförmigen Stange befestigt, können jedoch entlang der Rille, in die sie gesetzt sind, verschoben werden.

Les deux chambres d'enfants comportent un espace caché contenant un lavabo et un bidet. L'écran est mobile, parfaitement équilibré et absolument silencieux quand il pivote pour que l'on puisse utiliser les installations sanitaires, ou quand il est repoussé contre le mur pour agrandir la pièce.

Each of the two children's bedrooms has a screened area containing a basin and a bidet. The screen is mobile, perfectly balanced and absolutely silent as it pivots open for use of the facilities, or is pushed back against the wall to leave a greater sense of spaciousness in the room.

In den beiden Kinderschlafzimmern befindet sich jeweils ein durch Trennwände abgeteilter Bereich mit Waschbecken und Bidet. Die Trennwand ist beweglich, perfekt ausbalanciert und absolut geräuschlos: Zur Benutzung der Einrichtungen läßt sie sich mit einer Drehbewegung öffnen, sie kann aber auch an die Wand geschoben werden, damit der Raum größer wirkt.

La chambre du milieu, à l'origine conçue pour le fils des Dalsace, comporte un lit avec cadre métallique dont les pieds avant sont fixés à une barre attachée au mur par une charnière. Comme l'autre extrémité du lit repose simplement sur la partie surélevée du sol près des fenêtres, l'angle du lit par rapport au mur peut être modifié à volonté.

The middle bedroom, originally for the Dalsaces' son, has a metal frame bed, the front legs of which are fixed to a bar hinged to the wall. As the other end of the bed simply rests on the raised portion of the floor near the windows, the angle of the bed vis-à-vis the wall may be adjusted at will.

Im mittleren Schlafzimmer, ursprünglich für den Sohn der Dalsaces vorgesehen, befindet sich ein Bett mit Metallrahmen, dessen Beine auf der Vorderseite an einer mit Scharnieren an der Wand befestigten Stange angebracht sind. Da das andere Ende des Bettes lediglich auf einem erhöhten Teil des Bodens in der Nähe des Fensters steht, kann der Winkel des Bettes zur Wand beliebig verstellt werden.

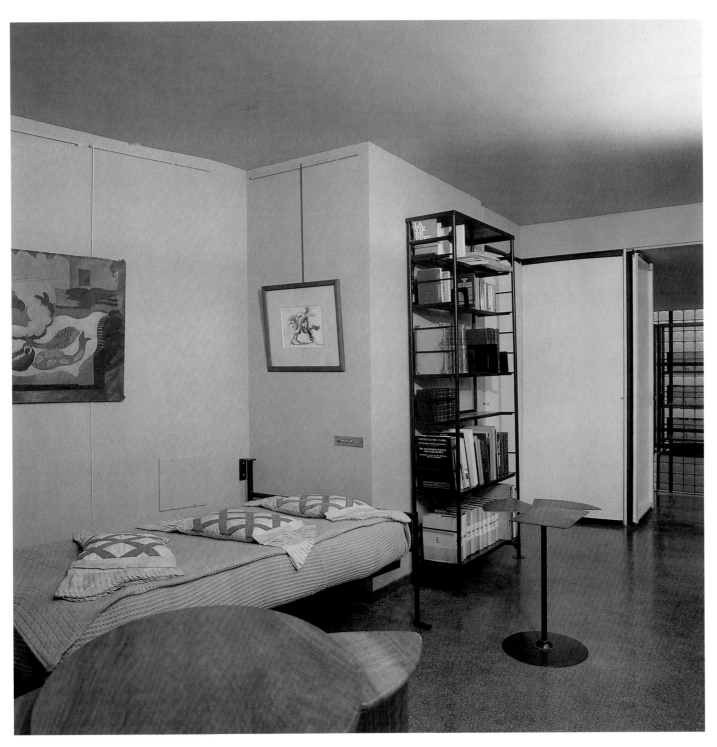

Les rayons à livres, la petite table en fer forgé (SN 9) et le lit comportent tous des éléments mobiles. Chareau excellait à créer des meubles qui, bien que déplaçables étaient incorporés à l'ensemble architectural.

The bookshelves, small wrought-iron table (SN 9) and bed all have mobile elements. Chareau excelled in creating furnishings which, although they could be moved in some way, were permanently fixed to the architectural ensemble.

Die Bücherregale sowie der kleine schmiedeeiserne Tisch (SN 9) und das Bett haben bewegliche Elemente. Chareau tat sich besonders hervor, indem er Einrichtungsgegenstände entwarf, die, obwohl sie auf irgendeine Art und Weise bewegt werden konnten, doch fest im architektonischen Ganzen verankert waren.

L'unité baignoire-bibliothèque de la salle de bains de la fille des Dalsace est un remarquable exemple de l'esprit inventif de Chareau. Les écrans métalliques perforés bouchent la baignoire quand on ne s'en sert pas; les livres peuvent être sortis des rayons sur des plateaux en métal et en verre – ils sont protégés à l'arrière par du verre armé.

A remarkable example of Chareau's inventiveness as an architectural and furniture designer is the bathtub-bookshelves unit in the Dalsace daughter's bathroom. The perforated sheet-metal screens close off the bathtub when not in use; the books can be taken from the shelves on metal and glass trays – they are protected from behind by reinforced glass.

Ein bemerkenswertes Beispiel für die Erfindungsgabe Chareaus als Innenarchitekt und Möbeldesigner ist die Badewannen-Bücherregal-Einheit im Badezimmer der Dalsaceschen Tochter. Die Trennwände aus Lochblech verdecken die Badewanne, wenn diese nicht benutzt wird; die Bücher können den Regalen auf Tabletts aus Metall und Glas entnommen werden – von hinten sind sie durch verstärktes Glas vor Nässe geschützt.

Un espace-bains caché, avec lavabo et bidet mobile, se trouve également dans la chambre de la fille. Ouvert ou fermé, l'écran mobile est à la fois une sorte de sculpture et un moyen pratique pour cacher un espace disgracieux utilisé pendant peu de temps chaque jour. La poésie et la fonction sont combinées dans un simple geste.

A screened washing area with basin and movable bidet is also present in the daughter's bedroom. Observed here in the open as well as closed position, the mobile screen is both a kind of sculpture and a practical means of concealing an unsightly space used for short periods every day. Poetry and utility are combined in a single gesture.

Ein durch Trennwände abgetrennter Waschbereich mit Waschbecken und beweglichem Bidet befindet sich ebenfalls im Schlafzimmer der Tochter. Betrachtet man hier die bewegliche Trennwand in geöffneter und in geschlossener Position, so zeigt sich, daß sie sowohl eine Art Skulptur ist als auch ein praktisches Mittel, um einen unansehnlichen Raum zu verbergen, der täglich nur für kurze Zeiträume benutzt wird. Poesie und Nützlichkeit sind somit in einer einzigen Bewegung vereint.

a

b

c

d

e

f

g

h

i

j

k

l

a) Détail d'escalier, Maison de Verre.

b) Roue permettant d'ouvrir les ventilateurs d'un côté de la façade principale en briques de verre, Maison de Verre.

c) Projecteur illuminant l'extérieur de la Maison de Verre.

d) Détail de colonne portante revêtue en acier, peinte et garnie de bandes en ardoise noire.

e) Plaque métallique perforée utilisée en panneaux pour couvrir certaines surfaces de la Maison de Verre.

f) Détail de panneaux de porte en métal et en verre menant à la terrasse, au deuxième étage de la Maison de Verre.

g) Porte-savon de la salle de bains principale de la Maison de Verre.

h) Portes ouvertes de la façade côté jardin.

i) Butoirs de porte spécialement conçus pour les portes donnant sur la terrasse de la Maison de Verre.

j) Etagère pivotante appelée «passe-plat», cachée dans le mur entre le petit salon et le couloir du garde-manger.

k) Les portes de placard en métal courbe au deuxième étage de la Maison de Verre ont une porte intérieure en bois conçue pour ranger les chaussures.

l) Coiffeuse semi-circulaire en verre et en acier tubulaire attachée par une charnière à la colonne, ce qui lui permet de pivoter sur une roulette conique.

a) Detail of stairs in the Maison de Verre.

b) Wheel for opening ventilators on one side of the main glass brick fasade in the Maison de Verre.

c) Spotlight illuminating the exterior of the Maison de Verre.

d) Detail of a rivetted steel structural column, painted and faced with black slate strips.

e) Perforated sheet iron used in panels to cover some surfaces in the Maison de Verre.

f) Detail of door panels of metal and glass leading to terrace on second floor of the Maison de Verre.

g) Soap dish in the master bathroom of the Maison de Verre.

h) Open doors in the garden façade.

i) Specially designed doorstops for doors to the terrace of the Maison de Verre.

j) Pivoting shelf called a »passe-plat« concealed in the wall between the small sitting room and pantry hallway.

k) Curved metal closet doors on the second floor of Maison de Verre have an inner wooden door fitted for storing shoes.

l) Semi-circular dressing table of glass and tubular steel attached by a hinge to the column, thereby allowing it to pivot on a conical roller.

a) Detail der Treppe in der Maison de Verre

b) Das Rad zum Öffnen der Lüftungsanlage befindet sich an einer Seite der Hauptglasbausteinfassade der Maison de Verre.

c) Scheinwerfer zur Außenbeleuchtung der Maison de Verre.

d) Detail eines Stahlkonstruktionspfeilers; der Pfeiler wurde bemalt und mit langen, schmalen Stücken aus schwarzem Schiefer verblendet.

e) Einige Flächen in der Maison de Verre wurden mit solchen Platten aus perforiertem Eisenblech verkleidet.

f) Detail der Türfüllungen aus Metall und Glas der Terrassentür im zweiten Stockwerk der Maison de Verre.

g) Seifenhalter im großen Badezimmer in der Maison de Verre.

h) Geöffnete Türen an der Gartenfassade.

i) Eigens für die Terrassentüren der Maison de Verre entworfene Türstopper.

j) Das als »passe-plat« bezeichnete schwenkbare Regalbrett ist in der Wand zwischen dem kleinen Wohnzimmer und dem Korridor in Höhe des Anrichteraums verborgen.

k) In den gewölbten Schranktüren aus Metall im zweiten Stockwerk der Maison de Verre befindet sich eine Holztür, die der Aufbewahrung von Schuhen dient.

l) Der halbkreisförmige Toilettentisch aus Glas und Stahlrohr ist mit einem Gelenk an einem Pfeiler befestigt, und läßt sich leicht auf einer konischen Rolle herausschwenken.

Pierre Chareau: 1883–1950

Vie et œuvre

Pierre Chareau, vers 1921

1883   Pierre Chareau est né le 3 août à Bordeaux d'Ester Carvallo et d'Adolphe Chareau. Son père, un négociant qui perdit ultérieurement sa fortune, alla s'installer avec sa famille à Paris où il trouva un emploi dans les Chemins de fer.

1899   A l'âge de 16 ans, Chareau est engagé comme dessinateur chez Waring & Gillow, une compagnie britannique installée à Paris et spécialisée dans les meubles et le design. Il rencontre Louise «Dollie» Dyte, une Anglaise de trois ans son aînée.

1904   Chareau épouse Dollie Dyte. Il continue à travailler chez Waring jusqu'en 1914, tandis que Dollie donne des leçons d'anglais. L'une de ses élèves est Annie Bernheim, la future femme du Docteur Jean Dalsace, le client le plus important de Chareau.

1914   Chareau est mobilisé pendant la Première Guerre mondiale.

1919   Après avoir passé plus de trois ans dans l'armée, Chareau est démobilisé. Il s'établit en tant que décorateur et concepteur de meubles à Paris. Parmi ses premières œuvres, le bureau et la chambre à coucher de l'appartement de Dalsace au 195, Boulevard St-Germain. Ses meubles sont exposés pour la première fois au Salon d'Automne.

1920   Il rencontre Jean Lurçat, le peintre cubiste et dessinateur de tapisseries, chez Edmund Bernheim (parents d'Annie Dalsace). Il décore l'appartement de Madeleine et Edmond Fleg, Quai aux Fleurs. Ses dessins de meubles et d'intérieur pour une chambre à coucher et une salle de bains sont exposés au Salon d'Automne et accueillis avec enthousiasme par la critique.

1921   Chareau devient membre permanent du comité d'organisation du Salon en 1921.

1922   Il expose pour la première fois au Salon des Artistes-Décorateurs. Il y rencontre des membres de l'Avant-Garde artistique et littéraire parisienne. Il se met à collectionner des œuvres de Modigliani, Braque, Juan Gris, Paul Klee, Max Ernst, Mondrian et d'autres encore.

1923   Collabore avec Fernand Léger et Robert Mallet-Stevens aux décors du film «L'inhumaine» de Marcel L'Herbier.

1924   Chareau ouvre son propre magasin appelé «La Boutique» au 3, rue du Cherche-Midi. C'est probablement à cette époque qu'il commence à collaborer avec Louis Dalbet, ferronnier spécialisé dans les créations en fer forgé. Les premiers fruits de leur collaboration sont présentés au Salon d'Automne.

1925   Il participe avec Mallet-Stevens et Francis Jourdain à la conception d'intérieurs et de meubles pour une «ambassade de France» destinée à l'Exposition Internationale des Arts Décoratifs et Industriels Modernes à Paris. Chareau y rencontre le jeune architecte néerlandais Bernard Bijvoët. Il réalise également son second film, «Le vertige», avec Marcel L'Herbier.

1926   Il se voit confier sa première mission architecturale: le pavillon d'un club à Beauvallon dans le Sud de la France pour Emile Bernheim (oncle d'Annie Dalsace). Il est secondé pour ce projet par Bijvoët.

1927   Ebauche les premiers plans d'une maison pour la famille Dalsace – qui deviendra plus tard la Maison de Verre – dans la rue St Guillaume à Paris.

1928   Chareau redécore l'intérieur du Grand Hotel de Tours. Est invité à participer aux Congrès Internationaux d'Architecture Moderne (CIAM) en juin à La Sarraz, Suisse. Les travaux de la Maison de Verre commencent, Chareau est assisté de Bijvoët et de Dalbet.

1929   Expose des meubles, la plupart en fer forgé, à l'exposition de la «Semaine à Paris». Rompt avec la Société des Artistes-Décorateurs pour devenir membre fondateur de l'Union des Artistes Modernes (UAM).

1930   Participe à la première exposition de l'Union des Artistes Modernes, qui a lieu au Musée des Arts Décoratifs à Paris.

1931   Est invité à devenir membre du comité de rédaction de la revue «L'Architecture d'Aujourd'hui» nouvellement créé. Est également membre des jurys de concours organisées par le même magazine. La presse nationale et internationale assure la couverture de la Maison de Verre qui est presque achevée.

1932   Rénove les bureaux de la compagnie des télégraphes et téléphones LTT, rue de la Faisanderie, Paris. Comme la récession économique mondiale est plus profondément ressentie en France après 1932, Chareau reçoit moins de commandes, que ce soit comme designer ou comme architecte.

1936   Expose des meubles scolaires démontables au Salon d'Automne.

1937   Expose à l'Exposition Universelle à Paris. Il dessine une petite maison de campagne en bois sur un terrain non loin de Rambouillet pour sa vieille amie, la danseuse Djémil Anik.

1939   Les derniers travaux de Chareau en France comprennent un projet pour l'administration coloniale. Il dessine des meubles faits à partir d'emballages en bois qui accompagnent les soldats outre-mer afin que ces derniers puissent construire des «foyers» dans leurs casernes.

1940   En juillet, Chareau quitte la France pour le Portugal via l'Espagne. Il se rend à Rabat et à Casablanca, au Maroc; là, il obtient un visa pour les Etats-Unis, où il arrive à la fin du mois d'octobre.

1941   Dollie Chareau rejoint son époux à New York. Ils y restent pendant toute la Deuxième Guerre mondiale. Chareau aide le département culturel de l'ambassade de France à organiser des expositions sur Balzac, Daumier, l'imagerie populaire et l'œuvre d'Auguste Perret.

1947   Chareau adapte une baraque militaire «Quonset» en métal à East Hampton, Long Island, et en fait une maison de week-end et studio pour son ami, le jeune peintre Robert Motherwell.

1948   L'architecte rénove une seconde maison de campagne d'une seule pièce pour Germaine Monteux et Nancy Laughlin.

1950   Pierre Chareau meurt à la suite d'une brève maladie. Dollie Chareau reste aux Etats-Unis jusqu'à sa mort.

Pierre Chareau: 1883–1950

Life and Work

Pierre Chereau, 1925

1883 Pierre Chareau is born in Bordeaux on 3 August to Ester Carvallo and Adolphe Chareau. His father, a »négociant« (merchant), subsequently loses his business, and moves with the family to Paris to work for the railways.

1899 At the age of 16, Chareau joins the Parisian offices of Waring & Gillow, a British firm specializing in furniture and interior design, as a tracing draughtsman. He meets Louise »Dollie« Dyte, an Englishwoman three years his senior.

1904 Chareau marries Dollie Dyte. He continues to work for Waring until 1914, while Dollie gives English lessons. One of her students is Annie Bernheim, future wife of Dr Jean Dalsace. They were to become Chareau's most important patrons.

1914 Conscripted for military service in the First World War.

1919 Having served over four years in the army, Chareau is demobilised. Establishes a practice as a private architect and furniture designer in Paris. Executes furniture and interiors for the offices and bedroom of the Dalsace apartment at 195 boulevard St Germain. His furniture is shown at the Salon d'Automne for the first time.

1920 Introduced to Jean Lurçat, the Cubist painter and tapestry designer, while decorating the country house of the Edmund Bernheims (parents of Annie Dalsace). Decorates the Fleg

apartment on the Quai aux Fleurs. His furniture designs and interiors for a bedroom and a bathroom are shown at the Salon d'Automne and attract critical acclaim.

1921 Chareau becomes a permanent member of the Salon organizing committee.

1922 Exhibits in the Salon des Artistes-Décorateurs for the first time. Meets members of the Parisian artistic and literary avant-garde, and begins collecting works by Modigliani, Braque, Juan Gris, Paul Klee, Raoul Dufy, Max Ernst, Mondrian and others.

1923 Collaborates with Fernand Léger and Robert Mallet-Stevens on the sets for Marcel L'Herbier's film »L'inhumaine«.

1924 Chareau opens his own shop, called »La Boutique«, at 3 rue du Cherche-Midi. He has by now begun working with Louis Dalbet, a metalwork craftsman specializing in art objects of wrought iron. First fruits of their collaboration are shown at the Salon d'Automne.

1925 Collaborates with Mallet-Stevens and Francis Jourdain on the interior designs and furnishings for a French Embassy for the Exposition Internationale des Arts Décoratifs et Industriels Modernes in Paris. Here Chareau also meets the young Dutch architect Bernard Bijvoët. Second film with Marcel L'Herbier, »Le vertige«.

1926 Chareau is awarded his first architectural commission: the Clubhouse in Beauvallon in southern France for Emile Bernheim (uncle of Annie Dalsace). He is assisted on the project by Bijvoët.

1927 First plans for a new house for the Dalsace family – what will become known as the Maison de Verre – in the rue St Guillaume in Paris.

1928 Refurbishment of the Grand Hotel de Tours in Tours. Participates in the Congrès International d'Architecture Moderne (CIAM) in La Sarraz, Switzerland, in June. Work begins on the Maison de Verre, for which Chareau is assisted by Bijvoët and Dalbet.

1929 Exhibits furniture, much of it made of wrought iron, at the »Semaine à Paris« show. Breaks away from the Société des Artistes-Décorateurs to become a founding member of the Union des Artistes Modernes (UAM).

1930 Participates in the first UAM exhibition, held at the Musée des Arts Décoratifs in Paris.

1931 Chareau is invited to join the editorial advisory board of the newly-created avant-garde »L'Architecture d'Aujourd'hui«. He also sits on the juries of competitions organized by the same magazine. The Maison de Verre receives wide coverage in both the national and international press as it nears completion.

1932 Renovates the offices of the LTT telephone and telegraph company in the rue de la Faisanderie, Paris. As the effects of the worldwide depression make themselves increasingly felt in France, the next few years see a decline in the number of Chareau's commissions, both for furniture designs and architectural projects.

1936 Exhibits demountable school furniture at the Salon d'Automne.

1937 Exhibits at the Exposition Universelle in Paris. Designs a small weekend house of wood for his long-time friend, the dancer Djémil Anik, on a site near Rambouillet.

1939 Chareau's last works in France include a commission from the colonial administration to design furniture which can be assembled from the packing crates accompanying soldiers overseas, enabling them to construct recreation spaces (foyers) in their barracks.

1940 In July Chareau leaves France for Portugal, via Spain. He travels on to Rabat and Casablanca, Morocco, where he obtains a visa for the USA. He arrives in America in late October.

1941 Dollie Chareau joins her husband in New York City, where they remain for the duration of World War II. Chareau works for the French Cultural Attaché, organising exhibitions on Balzac, Daumier, popular imagery and the work of Auguste Perret.

1947 Chareau converts a military Quonset hut into a weekend house and studio for his friend, the young painter Robert Motherwell, in East Hampton, Long Island.

1948 Renovates a one-room weekend house for Germaine Monteux and Nancy Laughlin.

1950 Pierre Chareau dies in New York after a brief illness. Dollie Chareau remains in the USA until her death in 1967.

Pierre Chareau: 1883–1950

Leben und Werk

Pierre Chareau, um 1935

1883 Pierre Chareau wird am 3. August als Sohn von Ester Carvallo und Adolph Chareau geboren. Sein Vater, ein Weinhändler, verliert später sein Vermögen und zieht mit seiner Familie nach Paris, wo er bei der Eisenbahn arbeitet.

1899 Mit sechzehn Jahren fängt Chareau bei Waring & Gillow, einer englischen Firma, die auf Möbel und Inneneinrichtung spezialisiert ist, als technischer Zeichner an. Er lernt die um drei Jahre ältere Engländerin Louise »Dollie« Dyte kennen.

1904 Chareau heiratet Dollie Dyte. Er arbeitet weiterhin für Waring & Gillow bis 1914, während dieser Zeit gibt Dollie Englischunterricht. Eine ihrer Schülerinnen ist Annie Bernheim, zukünftige Ehefrau von Dr. Jean Dalsace. Sie werden Chareaus wichtigste Mäzene.

1914 Einberufung zum Kriegsdienst im Ersten Weltkrieg.

1919 Nach vier Jahren wird Chareau aus dem Kriegsdienst entlassen. Macht sich als Architekt und Möbeldesigner in Paris selbständig. Entwirft und baut die Möbel und die Inneneinrichtung für die Praxisräume und das Schlafzimmer der Dalsaceschen Wohnung am Boulevard St. Germain Nr. 195. Seine Möbel werden zum erstenmal in der Ausstellung Salon d'Automne gezeigt.

1920 Als Chareau für das Ehepaar Edmund Bernheim (Eltern von Annie Dalsace) deren Landhaus renoviert, lernt er den kubistischen Maler und Designer für Dekorationsstoffen Jean Lurçat kennen. Chareau dekoriert die Wohnung für die Flegs am Quai aux Fleurs. Seine Möbelentwürfe und Inneneinrichtungen für ein Schlaf- und ein Badezimmer werden im Salon d'Automne gezeigt und finden den Beifall der Kritik.

1921 Chareau wird festes Mitglied des Organisationsausschusses des Salon.

1922 Stellt erstmals im Salon des Artistes-Décorateurs aus. Er lernt Mitglieder der Pariser Künstler- und Literatur-Avantgarde kennen und beginnt damit, Werke von Modigliani, Braque, Juan Gris, Paul Klee, Raoul Dufy, Max Ernst Mondrian und anderen zu sammeln.

1923 Zusammen mit Fernand Léger und Robert Mallet-Stevens arbeitet er an den Szenenaufbauten für Marcel L'Herbier's Film »L'inhumaine«.

1924 Chareau eröffnet sein eigenes Geschäft »La Boutique« in der Rue du Cherche-Midi. Er arbeitet jetzt bereits mit Louis Dalbet zusammen, einem Meisterschmied, der Kunstobjekte aus Schmiedeeisen herstellt. Erste Früchte ihrer Zusammenarbeit werden im Salon d'Automne gezeigt.

1925 Zusammen mit Mallet-Stevens und Francis Jourdain arbeitet er an der Inneneinrichtung und Ausstattung für eine französische Botschaft für die Exposition Internationale des Arts Décoratifs et Industrielles Modernes in Paris. Hier lernt Chareau auch den jungen niederländischen Architekten Bernard Bijvoët kennen. Zweiter Film mit Marcel L'Herbier, »Le vertige«.

1926 Chareau erhält seinen ersten Bauauftrag: das Klubhaus in Beauvallon in Südfrankreich für Emile Bernheim (Onkel von Annie Dalsace). Sein Assistent bei diesem Projekt ist Bijvoët.

1927 Erste Entwürfe für ein neues Haus für die Familie Dalsace – das später unter dem Namen Maison de Verre bekannt wird – in der Rue St. Guillaume in Paris.

1928 Neuausstattung des Grand Hotels de Tours in Tours. Im Juni Teilnahme am Congrès Internationaux d'Architecture Moderne (CIAM) in La Sarraz, Schweiz. Beginn der Bauarbeiten der Maison de Verre, Chareaus Assistenten bei diesem Projekt sind Bijvoët und Dalbet.

1929 Stellt Möbel auf der Ausstellung Semaine à Paris aus. Viele dieser Möbel sind aus Schmiedeeisen. Trennt sich von der Société des Artistes-Décorateurs und wird Gründungsmitglied der Union des Artistes Modernes (UAM).

1930 Teilnahme an der ersten UAM-Ausstellung im Musée des Arts Décoratifs in Paris.

1931 Chareau wird aufgefordert, dem redaktionellen Beratungsausschuß des erst kürzlich ins Leben gerufenen avantgardistischen Magazins »L'Architecture d'Aujourd'hui« anzugehören. Er sitzt auch in der Jury, die die Gewinner der Wettbewerbe ermittelt, die das Magazin veranstaltet. Über die Maison de Verre wird in der in- und ausländischen Presse ausführlich berichtet, als sie sich ihrer Vollendung nähert.

1932 Renoviert die Büroräume der LTT Telefon- und Telegraphengesellschaft in der Rue de la Faisanderie, Paris. Da die Auswirkungen der weltweiten Wirtschaftskrise in Frankreich in zunehmendem Maße spürbar werden, gehen in den nächsten paar Jahren sowohl Chareaus Aufträge für Möbelentwürfe als auch seine Bauaufträge zurück.

1936 Ausstellung von zerlegbaren Schulmöbeln im Salon d'Automne.

1937 Stellt auf der Exposition Universelle in Paris aus. Entwirft ein kleines Wochenendhaus aus Holz für seine langjährige Freundin, die Tänzerin Djémil Anik, auf einem Grundstück in der Nähe von Rambouillet.

1939 Zu Chareaus letzten Arbeiten in Frankreich gehört ein Auftrag der Kolonialverwaltung. Es handelt sich hierbei um den Entwurf von Transportkisten, die die Soldaten an ihrem Bestimmungsort in Übersee zur Einrichtung von Erholungsräumen (foyers) in ihren Baracken zu Möbeln zusammenbauen konnten.

1940 Im Juli verläßt Chareau Frankreich und geht über Spanien nach Portugal. Von da aus reist er weiter nach Rabat und Casablanca, Marokko, wo er ein Visum für die USA erhält. Im späten Oktober trifft er in den USA ein.

1941 Dollie Chareau kommt zu ihrem Mann nach New York, wo sie für die Dauer des Zweiten Weltkriegs bleiben. Chareau arbeitet für den französischen Kulturattaché als Organisator für Ausstellungen über Balzac, Daumier, populäre Bilder und das Werk von Auguste Perret.

1947 Für seinen Freund, den jungen Maler Robert Motherwell, baut Chareau in East Hampton, Long Island, eine Militärbaracke zu einem Wochenendhaus und Atelier um.

1948 Renoviert ein aus einem Raum bestehendes Wochenendhaus für Germaine Monteux und Nancy Laughlin.

1950 Pierre Chareau stirbt nach kurzer Krankheit in New York. Dollie Chareau bleibt bis zu ihrem Tod im Jahre 1967 in den USA.

Bibliographie

Textes isolés / Selected Works / Einzeldarstellungen

Brunhammer, Yvonne, *1925,* Presse de la connaissance, Paris 1976.

Futugawa, Yukio, editor and photographer, *La Maison de Verre / Pierre Chareau*. Texts by Bernard Bauchet and Marc Vellay, A.D.A. Edita, Tokyo 1988.

Futugawa, Yukio, editor and photographer, *Maison de Verre.* Text by Fernando Montes, Global Architecture, no. 46, A.D.A. Edita, Tokyo 1977.

Herbst, René (ed.), *Un Inventeur, l'Architecte Pierre Chareau,* Editions des Arts Ménagers, Paris 1954.

Vellay, Marc, *Pierre Chareau, Architecte Meublier, 1883–1950,* Editions Rivages, Paris 1986.

Vellay, Marc and Kenneth Frampton, *Pierre Chareau,* Editions du Regard, Paris 1984.

Velley, Marc, *Pierre Chareau, Architecte Meublier 1983–1950,* Rivages, Paris 1986.

Encyclopédie des Métiers d'Art. Décoration moderne, vol. I & II, Albert Morance, Paris n.d.

Articles/Artikel

Chareau, Pierre, «La Maison de Verre de Pierre Chareau commentée par lui-même», *Le point,* (Colmar) II, May 1937.

Chareau, Pierre, «Meubles, l'art international d'aujourd'hui» (Introduction), No.7, *Editions d'art Charles Moreau,* Paris n.d.

Fleg, Edmond, «Nos Décorateurs, Pierre Chareau», *Les Arts de la Maison,* winter 1924, pp. 17–27.

Saint-Cyr, Charles, «La première maison de verre...», *La Semaine à Paris,* 16 October 1931.

Duiker, J., «Het huis van Dr. d'Alsace in de Rue St. Guillaume te parijs», *OpBouw,* No. 18, 2 September 1933, pp. 155–64.

Frampton, Kenneth, «Maison de Verre», *Perspecta* (The Yale Architectural Journal), No. 12, 1969, pp. 77–126.

Frampton, Kenneth, «Maison de Verre», *Arena* (The Architectural Association Journal), Vol. 81, No. 901, pp. 257–62.

Rogers, Richard, «Pariji 1930», *Domus,* No. 443, October 1966, pp. 8–19.

Migennes, P., «Sur Deux Ensembles de P. Chareau», *Art et Décoration,* May 1932, pp. 129–140.

Janneau, G., «L'art décoratif», *Art et Décoration,* Novembre 1920, Vol. 38, pp. 141–60.

Varenne, G., «L'esprit moderne de Pierre Chareau», *Art et Décoration,* May 1923, Vol. 43, pp. 129–38.

L'architecture d'aujourd'hui, No. 9, 1933, articles by P. Vago, P. Nelson and J. Lepage, pp. 4–15.

George, W., «Les tendances générales», *l'Amour de l'Art,* No. 8, August 1925, pp. 283–91.

Velley, Marc, «Agli estremi del matone Nevada», *Rassegna,* No. 24 1985, pp. 6–17.

Velley, Marc, «An Insider's View», *House and Garden* (USA), February 1983, pp. 148–52.

Légendes

Les mesures se rapportent à la: hauteur (M), largeur (L), profondeur (P).

1 Lampadaire, vers 1920
Bois, albâtre et métal
H. min. 117 cm et max. 168 cm
Précurseur de la lampe SN31 appelée «La Religieuse»
Galerie Doria, Paris

2 Chaise (SN38), vers 1919
Acajou avec placage en ébène de Macassar
H. 110, L. 61, P. 46 cm
Collection privée, Paris

3 Guéridon (MB170), vers 1923
Sycomore, palissandre, ébène de Macassar, noyer ou acajou. Dessus de table hexagonal sur support en forme de tulipe avec six côtés sur socle hexagonal.
H. 61, L. 76, P. 76 cm
Galerie Vallois, Paris

4 Bergère (MF15), vers 1920–22
Noyer, hêtre, cuir, avec supports métalliques
H. 73, L. 66/74, P. 60 cm
Collection privée, Paris

5 Fauteuil (MF172), vers 1920
Palissandre et padouk, ou sycomore
Dossier gondole avec six panneaux inclinés, siège plein avec socle en bois massif.
H. 81, L. 77, P. 56 cm
Collection privée, Paris

6 Méridienne galbée (MP167), vers 1923
Palissandre, pieds en ivoire, velours
Dossier fait de quatre panneaux inclinés.
H. 81, L. 175, P. 85 cm
Collection privée, Paris

7 Fauteuil (MF220), vers 1922
Velours brun et noyer avec pieds métalliques en forme de boule
Dossier réglable, deux positions. Bois visible à l'avant et à l'arrière des accoudoirs. Les supports sous le siège sont verticaux, tournés en dehors au-dessus.
H. 80, L. 68, P. 79/84 cm
Collection privée, Paris

8 Fauteuil (MF158), vers 1928
Noyer et velours brun avec pieds métalliques en forme de boule
H. 74, L. 72, P. 79 cm
Collection privée, Genève

9 Canapé (MP158), vers 1928
Noyer et velours brun avec pieds métalliques en forme de boule
Siège long sans dossier. Accoudoirs inclinés devant et derrière.
H. 60, L. 187, P. 79 cm
Collection privée, Genève

10 Fauteuil (SN37), vers 1923
Palissandre et coussin recouvert de tissu
Pieds en bois moulé en forme de croix ou de lyre, accoudoirs et barres en bois apparent, dossier vertical.
H. 65, L. 74, P. 78 cm
Collection privée, Paris

11 Fauteuil avec dossier réglable (MF219), vers 1923
Palissandre ou noyer
Réglable, deux positions, à l'aide d'une barre mobile attachée avec des charnières, pieds en forme de lyre.
H. 93, L. 74, P. 95 cm
Collection privée, Paris

12 Table basse (MB130), vers 1924
Noyer et ronce de noyer, acajou de Cuba ou palissandre
Dessus de table ovale sur supports pleins avec petit tiroir et rayon intérieur. Deux ailes avec dessus triangulaire arrondi pivotant de chaque côté.
H. 55, L. 63, L. 47/98 cm
Collection privée, Paris

13 Table basse (MB106), vers 1924
Palissandre, palmier ou acajou avec charnière en bronze
Table composée de quatre surfaces triangulaires qui se déploient en éventail à partir d'un même axe.
H. 55/64, L. 66, P. 40 cm
Collection privée, Paris

14 Table (MB14), vers 1922/23
Chêne
Dessus de table ovale avec volets sur quatre pieds cylindriques fuselés reliés par des supports diagonaux, avec tiroir filets coulissante
H. 74, dessus de table 120 × 84 cm
Collection privée, Paris

15 Lit d'enfant, 1923
Chêne et cuivre
Deux extrémités massives, deux côtés munis de barreaux de bois, dont l'un peut être rabattu. Entièrement démontable.
Conçu à l'origine pour les enfants Dalsace.
H. 96, L. 135, P. 69 cm
Collection privée, Paris

16 Fauteuil en bois, 1923
Chêne
Partie de l'ensemble de la nursery Dalsace.
H. 97, L. 53, P. 43 cm
Collection privée, Paris

17 Chaise, 1923
Chêne
Haut dossier droit composé de deux fins éléments courbes qui se prolongent pour former les pieds arrière de la chaise, et un panneau central massif.
Il existe plusieurs versions, dont l'une comporte un siège bas pour femmes qui allaitent.
H. 98, L. 39, P. 37 cm
Collection privée, Paris

18 Table à langer, 1923
Chêne
Spécialement conçue pour changer les bébés, avec dossier et côtés pour empêcher le bébé de tomber.
H. 95, L. 70, P. 62 cm
Collection privée, Paris

19 Lampe de table, vers 1924
Noyer, albâtre et métal
Socle conique en bois avec abat-jour fait de quatre plaques triangulaires en albâtre disposées au-dessus du socle et maintenues par des pinces métalliques.
Dimensions inconnues
Galerie Vallois, Paris

20 Lampe de table (LP180), 1922
Métal et albâtre
Socle composé d'une bande de fer forgé repliée sur elle-même à la base et en haut, avec un abat-jour fait de deux morceaux d'albâtre fixés par des supports métalliques et suspendus à la partie fixe de la lampe.
H. 28,5, L. 25, P. 22 cm
Collection privée, Paris

21 Lampe de table, vers 1923
Bois, albâtre
Abat-jour composé de 4 morceaux d'albâtre, tous ajustables
H. 90 cm
Galerie Vallois, Paris

22 Lampadaire (SN31), 1923
Acajou de Cuba, albâtre et cuivre
Support conique en bois avec abat-jour fait de quatre plaques triangulaires en albâtre maintenues par des pinces en cuivre.
H. 186 cm
Galerie Vallois, Paris

23 Applique, vers 1923
Métal nickelé et albâtre
Neuf plaques d'albâtre maintenues par du métal nickelé.
H. 24, L. 57, P. 18 cm
Collection Musée d'Art Moderne de la Ville de Paris

24 Fauteuil à dossier haut (MF1002), 1924–27
Charpente recouverte de tapisserie conçue par J. Lurçat (restaurée conformément au carton original).
H. 95, L. 69, P. 44 cm
Collection privée, Paris

25 Sofa-canapé (MP169), 1923
Velours et tapisserie conçue par J. Lurçat
Long siège ovale entouré d'un dossier bas arrondi aux extrémités pour former des accoudoirs.
H. 57/60, L. 192/197, P. 83 cm
Collection privée, Paris

26 Tabouret (MT1015), vers 1923
Acajou
Type curule, siège concave, supports latéraux massifs reposant sur quatre parallélépipèdes.
H. 35/46, L. 50, P. 33 cm
Galerie Vallois, Paris

27 Sofa-canapé (MP287), 1924
Noyer et tissu
Dossier légèrement courbe, côtés évasés, coins arrondis sur le devant, le tout reposant sur des pieds métalliques en forme de boule.
H. 68,5, L. 212, P. 87 cm
Galerie Arc-en-Seine, Paris

28 Bureau (MB212), 1925
Placage de palissandre sur acajou et chêne
Surface de travail plane entre deux surfaces inclinées comportant des casiers fermant à clé, fond incliné relevé contenant un classeur de lettres mobile recouvert de peau de porc derrière deux volets à glissières, porté devant par deux socles avec trois tiroirs de chaque côté et deux placards séparés ouvrant sur le côté. Poignées en acier poli.
H. 76, L. 140, L. 77 cm
Collection Musée des Arts Décoratifs, Paris

29 Table de jeux pliante (MB241), vers 1929
Noyer, bronze et cuivre
Longue surface étroite avec extrémités arrondies sur lesquelles repose une surface carrée avec quatre abattants triangulaires que l'on peut déplier pour former une surface carrée plus grande. Les pieds sont situés de chaque côté de la longue surface, pivotent sur des charnières de bronze pour porter les abattants. Des cendriers en cuivre sont incorporés à chaque extrémité de la longue surface.
H. 65/69, L. 145, L. 52 cm
Collection privée, Paris

30 Bureau (MB1055), vers 1926
Sycomore
Surface de travail rectangulaire avec surfaces latérales inclinées qui s'ouvrent et découvrent des réceptacles peu profonds.
H. 69, L. 125, P. 50 cm
Collection privée, Paris

31 Coiffeuse (MS1009), 1926/27
Noyer
Surface basse en forme de J reposant sur une colonne composée de trois tiroirs à gauche, et un support vertical massif sur la droite.
H. 53,5, L. 95, P. 74,5 cm
Collection privée, Paris

32 Bureau (MB673), vers 1927
Palissandre et fer forgé
Surface de travail en forme de L encadrée de bandes de fer forgé. Sur la droite, des pieds métalliques supportent une étagère rectangulaire au-dessus de la surface de travail à laquelle est suspendu un petit meuble. Sur la gauche se trouve une console pivotante pour le téléphone.
H. 83,5, L. 161,5, P. 103,5 cm
Collection privée, Paris

33 Tabouret (SN3), vers 1927
Palissandre ou acajou avec métal ou fer forgé
Siège en bois avec supports métalliques.

H. 46/49, L. 49, P. 38 cm
Collection privée, Paris

34 Ensemble coiffeuse et tabouret (MS423 & MT1015), vers 1926/27
Sycomore et métal argenté
Dessus de table rectangulaire avec centre légèrement renfoncé et avant bombé. Supports latéraux massifs. Miroir inclinable avec appareils d'éclairage ajustables qui illuminent le miroir ou l'usager. Tabouret en sycomore (voir également **26 Tabouret (MT1015), vers 1923**).
Dimensions inconnues
Galerie Doria, Paris

35 Coiffeuse avec meuble pour cosmétiques (MS418), vers 1927
Sycomore et fer forgé
Comprend deux éléments à charnières, un miroir entièrement encadré de bois sur la droite, un meuble avec dessus de table fixe et une planche pivotante sur la gauche; chaque pièce est individuellement encadrée de fer forgé, l'ensemble repose sur trois pieds en fer forgé.
H. 166/116, L. 66/95, P. 9/30 cm
Collection Musée d'Art Moderne de la Ville de Paris, Paris

36 Table de bureau (MT876), vers 1929
Métal et bois recouvert de cuir rouge
Table pour machines à écrire et à calculer. Deux unités: à droite, une surface rectangulaire fixe et un support latéral portant un meuble métallique avec porte courbe s'ouvrant vers le bas; à gauche, une surface de travail pivotante sur des supports en fer forgé.
H. 60, L. 155, P. 40 cm
Collection privée, Paris

37 Coffre à linge (MA373), vers 1927
Ronce de noyer avec intérieur en sycomore.
Coffre supporté par des bandes métalliques l'entourant sur trois côtés. Contient trois planches et huit tiroirs d'un côté, quinze petits compartiments et cinq petits tiroirs de l'autre.
H. 99, L. 70, P. 40 cm
Collection privée, Paris

38 Armoire, vers 1923
Chêne
Armoire composée de trois portes à un seul panneau et de quatre tiroirs reposant sur quatre pieds en forme de boule.
H. 148, L. 158, P. 48 cm
Collection privée, Paris

39 Table basse (MB152), vers 1925
Série de quatre tables triangulaires en bois pivotant à partir d'une seule colonne; la partie supérieure évidée peut être utilisée comme bibliothèque.
Total H. 81, Table H. 56, L. 61, P. 37,5, 31, 29 et 26 cm
Galerie Vallois, Paris

40 Fauteuil club (MF313), vers 1926
Velours, tapisserie ou cuir
Dossier avec coussin en forme de fuseau à une extrémité.
H. 57, L. 90 cm
Collection privée, Paris

41 Chaise (MF276), vers 1924
Noyer, sycomore, palissandre, chêne ou hêtre teinté, et siège en cuir ou en tissu
Dossier vertical courbe, pieds fuselés en sycomore, siège recouvert de tissu.
H. 86, L. 52, P. 42 cm
Collection privée, Paris

42 Tabourets de bar (MT344), 1926
Bois et métal
Siège concave en bois massif sur pieds en tubes de métal reposant sur boules de bois.
H. 88, siège 35 × 35 cm
Galerie Arc-en-Seine, Paris

43 Table de jeux, vers 1928
Bois et métal
Dessus de table carré avec coins arrondis. Panneaux plats avec cavité pour verre ou cendrier creusée en diagonale par rapport à chaque coin. Le dessus de table repose sur des pieds en tubes de métal, des supports métalliques permettant le déplacement de la table.

H. 73, dessus de table 79 × 79 cm
Galerie Doria, Paris

44 Table, vers 1927
Bois massif et fer forgé
Dessus de table taillé dans un rectangle en bois massif sur des pieds en fer forgé fixés à chaque extrémité par des barres métalliques posées sur des sphères métalliques, tenant compte de la mobilité.
H. 47,5, L. 120, L. 70 cm
Galerie Vallois, Paris

45 Chaise (MC767), vers 1927
Métal et osier
Dossier droit avec siège convexe, tous deux en vannerie, encastrés dans de minces supports métalliques.
H. 80, L. 35, P. 55 cm
Collection privée, Paris

46 Table basse en tubes et en verre, vers 1932
Tubes en duralumin et verre
Deux dessus de table portés par des tubes en duralumin, courbés et soudés pour former un T en bas; le grand dessus de table semi-circulaire en verre est fixé à trois pieds, le petit dessus de table semi-circulaire en verre repose sur deux supports soudés.
H. 60, L. 62, P. 63 cm
Epaisseur du verre: 2,1 cm
Collection privée, Paris

Captions

The measurements refer to: height (H), width (W), depth (D), length (L).

1 Floor Lamp, c. 1920
Wood, alabaster and metal
H. min. 117 cm and max. 168 cm
Precursor to the lamp SN31 called »The Nun«
(»La Religieuse«)
Galerie Doria, Paris

2 Chair (SN38), c. 1919
Mahogany with veneer of macassar ebony
H. 110, W. 61, D. 46 cm
Private collection, Paris

3 Pedestal Table (MB170), c. 1923
Sycamore, rosewood, macassar ebony, walnut or mahogany
Hexagonal top over tulip shaped stand with six sides on hexagonal base
H. 61, L. 76, W. 76 cm
Galerie Vallois, Paris

4 Chair »Bergère« (MF15), c. 1920–22
Walnut, beech, leather, with metallic struts
H. 73, W. 66/74, D. 60 cm
Private collection, Paris

5 Armchair (MF172), c. 1920
Rosewood and padouk or sycamore
Gondola back with six sloping panels, full seat with solid wood base
H. 65, W. 77, D. 56 cm
Private collection, Paris

6 Curved Sofa »Méridienne galbée« (MP167), c. 1923
Rosewood, ivory feet, velours
Gondola back rest with four sloping panels
H. 81, L. 175, W. 85 cm
Private collection, Paris

7 Armchair (MF220), c. 1922
Brown velours and walnut with metal bun feet
Back adjusts to two positions. Visible wood at front and back of armrests. Supports below seat are upright, splay out above
H. 80, W. 68, D. 79/84 cm
Private collection, Paris

8 Armchair (MF158), c. 1928
Walnut and brown velours with metal bun feet
H. 74, W. 72, D. 79 cm
Private collection, Geneva

9 Couch (MP158), c. 1928
Walnut and brown velours with metal bun feet
Long seat with sloping armrests on either side
H. 60, W. 187, D. 79 cm
Private collection, Geneva

10 Armchair (SN37), c. 1923
Rosewood and cushion covered with fabric
Cruciform or lyre-shaped moulded wooden legs, exposed wooden arms, crossbars and back upright
H. 65, W. 74, D. 78 cm
Private collection, Paris

11 Armchair with Reclining Back (MF219), c. 1923
Rosewood or walnut
Adjusts to two positions by means of moving bar attached with hinges, with lyre-shaped legs
H. 93, W. 74, D. 95 cm
Private collection, Paris

12 Low Table (MB130), c. 1924
Walnut and knotted walnut, Cuban mahogany or rosewood

Oval top on full floor stand with small drawer and inside shelf. Two wings with rounded triangular tops pivot out from either side
H. 55, L. 63, W. 47/98 cm
Private collection, Paris

13 Low Table (MB106), c. 1924
Rosewood, palm wood or mahogany with bronze hinge
Table composed of four triangular surfaces which fan out from a single axis
H. 55/64, L. 66, W. 40 cm
Private collection, Paris

14 Table (MB14), c. 1922/23
Oak
Oval drop-leaf tabletop on four cylindrical tapered legs linked by diagonal struts, with sliding net drawers on either side
H. 74, Tabletop 120 × 84 cm
Private collection, Paris

15 Child's Bed, 1923
Oak and brass
Two solid ends with two wooden barred sides, one of which can be lowered. Entirely demountable. Originally designed for the Dalsace children
H. 96, L. 135, D. 69 cm
Private collection, Paris

16 Wooden Armchair, 1923
Oak
Part of the Dalsace nursery ensemble
H. 97, W. 53, D. 43 cm
Private collection, Paris

17 Chair, 1923
Oak
A high straight back comprising two slender curved elements, which extend to form the rear legs of the chair, and a solid central panel. Several versions exist, one of which has a low seat designed to accommodate nursing mothers.
H. 98, W. 39, D. 37 cm
Private collection, Paris

18 Nursery dressing table, 1923
Oak
Designed especially for changing babies, with raised back and sides to prevent a baby from falling off
H. 95, L. 70, W. 62 cm
Private collection, Paris

19 Table Lamp, c. 1924
Walnut, alabaster and metal
Conical wooden base with shade consisting of four triangular plaques of alabaster arranged above the base, held in place with metal clips
Dimensions unknown
Galerie Vallois, Paris

20 Table Lamp (LP180), 1922
Metal and alabaster
Base composed of a triangular strip of wrought metal folded in upon itself at the base and the top, with shade consisting of two pieces of alabaster fixed together by metal brackets, suspended from the light fixture
H. 28.5, W. 25, D. 22 cm
Private collection, Paris

21 Table Lamp, c. 1923
Wood, alabaster
Shade composed of four pieces of alabaster, all adjustable
H. 90 cm
Galerie Vallois, Paris

22 Floor Lamp (SN31), 1923
Cuban mahogany, alabaster and brass
Wooden conical stand with shade made with four triangular alabaster plaques held by brass clips
H. 186 cm
Galerie Vallois, Paris

23 Wall Lamp, c. 1923
Nickel-plated metal and alabaster
Nine plaques of alabaster held in place with nickel-plated metal

H. 24, W. 57, D. 18 cm
Collection Musée d'Art Moderne de la Ville de Paris

24 High-backed Armchair (MF1002), 1924–27
Frame covered with tapestry designed by J. Lurçat (restored according to the original cartoon)
H. 95, W. 69, D. 44 cm
Private collection, Paris

25 Couch (Sofa canapé) (MP169), 1923
Velours and tapestry designed by J. Lurçat
Long oval seat, enclosed by a low level back which curves at the ends to form armrests
H. 57/60, W. 192/197, D. 83 cm
Private collection, Paris

26 Stool (MT1015), c. 1923
Mahogany
Curule type, concave seat, solid side supports, resting on four parallel epipeds
H. 35/46, W. 50, D. 33 cm
Galerie Vallois, Paris

27 Couch (MP287), 1924
Walnut and fabric
Back slightly curved, sides flared out, curved angles in front, the whole resting on metal bun feet
H. 68.5, W. 212, D. 87 cm
Galerie Arc en Seine, Paris

28 Desk (MB212), 1925
Rosewood veneer on mahogany and oak
Flat top between two sloping surfaces which conceal lockers, raised inclined back containing removable letter file covered in pigskin behind two sliding flaps, and supported in front by two pedestals with three drawers on either side and two detached side-opening cupboards behind. Polished steel handles
H. 76, L. 140, W. 77 cm
Collection Musée des Arts Décoratifs, Paris

29 Folding Games Table (MB241), c. 1929
Walnut, bronze and brass
Long narrow surface with rounded ends on which rests a square surface with four triangular leaves, which fold out to form a larger square surface. Legs on either side of the long surface pivot out on bronze hinges to support the leaves. Brass ashtrays are incorporated at either end of the long surface
H. 65/69, L. 145, W. 52 cm
Private collection, Paris

30 Writing Table (MB1055), c. 1926
Sycamore
Rectangular work plane with lateral sloping surfaces which slide open to disclose shallow receptacles
H. 69, W. 125, D. 50 cm
Private collection, Paris

31 Dressing Table (MS1009), 1926/27
Walnut
Low J-shaped surface resting on a column of three drawers to the left, solid upright support on the right
H. 53.5, W. 95, D. 74.5 cm
Private collection, Paris

32 Desk (MB673), c. 1927
Rosewood and wrought iron
An L-shaped work surface encased in wrought-iron strips. On the right, wrought-iron legs extend to support a rectangular shelf above the work surface from which a small cabinet is also suspended. On the left is a cantilevered pivoting shelf for a telephone
H. 83.5, W. 161.5, D. 103.5 cm
Private collection, Paris

33 Stool (SN3), c. 1927
Rosewood or mahogany with metal or wrought iron
Wooden seat with metal supports
H. 46/49, W. 49, D. 38 cm
Private collection, Paris

34 Dressing Table and Stool Ensemble (MS423 & MT1015), c. 1926/27
Sycamore and silvered metal
Rectangular top with slightly sunken centre and bow front.

Solid side supports. Inclining mirror with adjustable light fittings that illuminate mirror or user. Stool in sycamore (see also **26 Stool (MT1015), c. 1923**)
Dimensions unknown
Galerie Doria, Paris

35 Dressing Table with Cosmetic Cabinet (MS418), c. 1927
Sycamore and wrought iron
Comprising two hinged elements, a full-length wooden-framed mirror on the right, cabinet with fixed tabletop and pivoting shelf on the left, each individually framed in wrought iron, and the whole resting on three wrought-iron legs
H. 166/116, W. 66/95, D. 9/30 cm
Collection Musée d'Art Moderne de la Ville de Paris, Paris

36 Office Table (MT876), c. 1929
Metal and wood covered with red leather
Table for typewriters and calculators. Two units; at right a fixed rectangular surface and side support bearing a metal cabinet with a curved door that opens downwards; to the left, a pivoting work surface resting on wrought-iron supports
H. 60, W. 155, D. 40 cm
Private collection, Paris

37 Linen Chest (MA373), c. 1927
Knotted walnut with sycamore interior
Box chest supported by wrought-iron strips that enclose it on three sides. Contains three shelves and eight drawers on one side, fifteen small compartments and five shallow drawers on the other
H. 99, W. 70, D. 40 cm
Private collection, Paris

38 Armoire, c. 1923
Oak
Wardrobe consisting of three single-panel doors and four drawers resting on four ball-shaped feet
H. 148, W. 158, D. 48 cm
Private collection, Paris

39 Low Table (MB152), c. 1925
Nest of four wooden triangular-shaped tables, pivots out from a single column, the hollow upper area of which can be used as a bookcase
Total H. 81, Table H. 56.5, W. 61, D. 37.5, 31, 29 and 26 cm
Galerie Vallois, Paris

40 Fireside Chair (MF313), c. 1926
Velours, tapestry or leather
Bolster back tapered at one end
H. 57, W. 90 cm
Private collection, Paris

41 Chair (MF276), c. 1924
Walnut, sycamore, rosewood, oak or stained beech, and leather or fabric seat
Curved upright back, tapered legs of sycamore, seat covered in fabric
H. 86, W. 52, D. 42 cm
Private collection, Paris

42 Bar Stools (MT344), 1926
Wood and metal
Concave seat in solid wood on tubular metal legs standing on round wooden feet
H. 88, Seat 35 × 35 cm
Galerie Arc en Seine, Paris

43 Games Table, c. 1928
Wood and metal
Square tabletop with rounded corners. Flat panels, featuring a hole for holding a glass or ashtray, pull out diagonally from each corner. The tabletop rests on tubular metal legs with round feet; curved metal struts form arches between these legs
H. 73, Tabletop 79 × 79 cm
Galerie Doria, Paris

44 Table, c. 1927
Solid wood and wrought iron
Solid wooden rectangular bevelled top on wrought-iron legs, linked at each end by a metal bar resting on metal spheres which allows for mobility

H. 47.5, L. 120, W. 70 cm
Galerie Vallois, Paris

45 Chair (MC767), c. 1927
Metal and wicker
Straight back with convex seat, both of wicker, framed in thin metal supports
H. 80, W. 35, D. 55 cm
Private collection, Paris

46 Low Tubular and Glass Table, c. 1932
Duralumin tubes and glass
Two tabletops, supported by duralumin tubes, bent and welded to form a T at the bottom, the large semicircular glass top screwed to three legs, the small semicircular glass top resting on two welded brackets
H. 60, W. 62, D. 63 cm
Thickness of glass: 2,1 cm
Private collection, Paris

Legenden

Die Maßangaben beziehen sich auf: Höhe (H), Breite (B), Tiefe (T), Länge (L).

1 Stehlampe, um 1920
Holz, Alabaster und Metall
H. min. 117 cm und max. 168 cm
Vorläufer der Lampe SN31, genannt »Die Nonne«
(»La Religieuse«)
Galerie Doria, Paris

2 Stuhl (SN38), um 1919
Mahagoni mit Furnier aus Makassar-Ebenholz
H. 110, B. 61, T. 46 cm
Privatsammlung, Paris

3 Tisch mit Säulenfuß (MB170), um 1923
Sykomore, Palisander, Makassar-Ebenholz, Nußbaum
oder Mahagoni
Sechseckige Platte über tulpenförmigem Säulenfuß mit
sechs Seiten auf sechseckiger Standplatte
H. 61, L. 76, B. 76 cm
Galerie Vallois, Paris

4 Sessel »Bergère« (MF15), um 1920–22
Nußbaum, Buche, Leder, mit Querverstrebung aus Metall
H. 63, B. 66/74, T. 60 cm
Privatsammlung, Paris

5 Armsessel (MF172), um 1920
Palisander und Padouk, oder Sykomore
Gondelförmige Rückenlehne mit sechs schrägen Platten,
stabiles Holzgestell mit Vollpolsterung
H. 65, B. 77, T. 56 cm
Privatsammlung, Paris

**6 Geschwungenes Sofa »Méridienne Galbée«
(MP167), um 1923**
Palisander, Elfenbeinfüße, Velours
Gondelförmige Rückenlehne mit vier schrägen Platten
H. 81, L. 175, B. 85 cm
Privatsammlung, Paris

7 Armlehnsessel (MF220), um 1922
Brauner Velours und Nußbaum mit knotenförmigen Füßen
aus Metall
Rückenlehne zweifach verstellbar. Holz sichtbar auf der
Vorder- und Rückseite der Armlehnen. Seitenteile unter-
halb der Sitzfläche gerade, oberhalb abgeschrägt
H. 80, B. 68, T. 79/84 cm
Privatsammlung, Paris

8 Sessel (MF158), um 1928
Nußbaum und brauner Velours mit knotenförmigen Füßen
aus Metall
H. 74, B. 72, T. 79 cm
Privatsammlung, Genf

9 Couch (MP158), um 1928
Nußbaum und brauner Velours mit knotenförmigen Füßen
aus Metall
Lange Sitzfläche mit abgeschrägten Armlehnen auf beiden
Seiten
H. 60, B. 187, T. 79 cm
Privatsammlung, Genf

10 Sessel (SN37), um 1923
Palisander und stoffbezogene Kissen
Kreuzförmige oder gebogene Beine aus Holz. Die Armleh-
nen, Querverstrebungen und hinteren Stützen sind aus
nacktem Holz.
H. 65, B. 74, T. 78 cm
Privatsammlung, Paris

**11 Sessel mit verstellbarer Rückenlehne (MF219),
um 1923**
Palisander oder Nußbaum

Zweifach verstellbar durch bewegliche, an Gelenken be-
festigte Stange. Gebogene Beine
H. 93, B. 74, T. 95 cm
Privatsammlung, Paris

12 Niedriger Tisch (MB106), um 1924
Nußbaum und Augennußbaum, kubanisches Mahagoni
oder Palisander
Ovale Platte auf massivem Gestell mit kleiner Schublade
und Regalbrett. Zwei beidseitig herausdrehbare Seiten-
teile mit abgerundeten, dreieckigen Platten
H. 55, L. 63, B. 47/98 cm
Privatsammlung, Paris

13 Niedriger Tisch (MB106), um 1924
Palisander, Palmenholz oder Mahagoni mit Bronze-
scharnier
Der Tisch besteht aus vier dreieckigen Flächen, die sich
von einer einzigen Achse aus fächerförmig ausbreiten.
H. 55/64, L. 66, B. 40 cm
Privatsammlung, Paris

14 Tisch (MB14), um 1922/23
Eiche
Ovale Tischplatte mit herunterklappbaren Seitenteilen auf
vier verjüngten Rundbeinen, die durch Diagonalverstre-
bungen miteinander verbunden sind. Auf beiden Seiten
befinden sich herausziehbare Aufbewahrungsnetze.
H. 74, Tischplatte 120 × 84 cm
Privatsammlung, Paris

15 Kinderbett, 1923
Eiche und Messing
Stabiles Kopf- und Fußteil mit zwei hölzernen Gitterseiten,
von denen eine niedriger gestellt werden kann. Komplett
zerlegbar. Ursprünglich entworfen für die Kinder der
Dalsaces
H. 96, L. 135, T. 69 cm
Privatsammlung, Paris

16 Armlehnstuhl aus Holz, 1923
Eiche
Teil der Dalsaceschen Kinderzimmereinrichtung
H. 97, B. 53, T. 43 cm
Privatsammlung, Paris

17 Stuhl, 1923
Eiche
Die hohe, gerade Rückenlehne besteht aus zwei schlanken, gebogten Elementen, deren Verlängerungen die Hin-
terbeine des Stuhles bilden, und einer massiven Holzplatte
in der Mitte. Von diesem Stuhl gibt es mehrere Varianten,
darunter eine mit niedrigem Sitz für stillende Mütter.
H. 98, B. 39, T. 37 cm
Privatsammlung, Paris

18 Wickeltisch, 1923
Eiche
Der in erster Linie als Wickeltisch entworfene Tisch hat
einen Aufsatz, damit das Baby beim Wickeln nicht her-
unterfällt.
H. 95, L. 70, B. 62 cm
Privatsammlung, Paris

19 Tischlampe, um 1924
Nußbaum, Alabaster und Metall
Kegelförmiger Lampenfuß aus Holz mit Schirm, beste-
hend aus vier dreieckigen Alabasterplatten. Die Platten
sind über dem Fuß angeordnet und werden von Halterun-
gen aus Metall gehalten
Maße unbekannt
Galerie Vallois, Paris

20 Tischlampe (LP180), 1922
Metall und Alabaster
Das Gestell besteht aus einem dreieckigen, schmalen
Stück Schmiedeeisen, das oben und unten in sich selbst
gefaltet ist. Der an der Lampenvorrichtung aufgehängte
Schirm besteht aus zwei Alabasterstücken, die mit Metall-
haltern zusammengehalten werden.
H. 28,5, B. 25, T. 22 cm
Privatsammlung, Paris

21 Tischlampe, um 1923
Holz, Alabaster
Der Schirm besteht aus vier beweglichen Alabaster-
platten.

H. 90 cm
Galerie Vallois, Paris

22 Stehlampe (SN31), 1923
Kubanisches Mahagoni, Alabaster und Messing
Kegelförmiger Lampenfuß aus Holz mit Schirm aus vier
dreieckigen Alabasterplatten, die von Halterungen aus
Messing gehalten werden
H. 186 cm
Galerie Vallois, Paris

23 Wandlampe, um 1923
Vernickeltes Metall und Alabaster
Neun Alabasterplatten, gehalten von vernickeltem Metall
H. 24, B. 57, T. 18 cm
Sammlung Musée d'Art Moderne de la Ville de Paris, Paris

24 Sessel mit hoher Rückenlehne (MF1002), 1924–27
Rahmen bezogen mit von J. Lurçat entworfenem Gobelin
(rekonstruiert nach Originalentwurf)
H. 95, B. 69, T. 44 cm
Privatsammlung, Paris

25 Couch (Sofa Kanapee) (MP169), 1923
Velours und von J. Lurçat entworfener Gobelin
Lange, ovale Sitzfläche, umgeben von einer niedrigen
Rückenlehne, deren geschwungene Enden die Armlehnen
bilden
H. 57/60, L. 192/197, T. 83 cm
Privatsammlung, Paris

26 Hocker (MT1015), um 1923
Mahagoni
Der auf vier Stollenfüßen stehende Hocker erinnert an
einen altrömischen Faltstuhl. Konkav geformter Sitz,
seitliche Stützen aus Massivholz
H. 35/46, B. 50, T. 87 cm
Galerie Vallois, Paris

27 Couch (MP287), 1924
Nußbaum und Stoff
Leicht geschwungene Rückenlehne, ausgestellte Seiten-
teile, Kanten vorne abgerundet. Die Couch steht auf kno-
tenförmigen Metallfüßen.
H. 68,5, L. 212, T. 87 cm
Galerie Arc en Seine, Paris

28 Schreibtisch (MB212), 1925
Palisanderfurnier auf Mahagoni oder Eiche
Ebene Arbeitsfläche zwischen zwei schräg abfallenden
Flächen, die Schließfächer verdecken. Der hintere Teil der
Tischplatte ist erhöht mit nach innen geneigten Flächen.
Hier befinden sich hinter zwei Schiebeklappen abnehm-
bare Briefordner aus Schweinsleder. Vorne wird die Platte
von zwei Unterschränken mit je drei Schubfächern getra-
gen und hinten von zwei einzelnen, von der Seite zu öffn-
enden Schränken. Handgriffe aus poliertem Stahl
H. 76, L. 140, B. 77 cm
Sammlung Musée des Arts Decoratifs, Paris

29 Zusammenklappbarer Spieltisch (MB241), um 1929
Nußbaum, Bronze und Messing
Lange, schmale, an den Enden abgerundete Fläche, auf
der eine quadratische Fläche mit vier dreieckigen Zusatz-
platten ruht, die auseinandergeklappt eine größere quadra-
tische Fläche bilden. Um die Platten zu stützen, lassen sich
die an beiden Seiten der schmalen Fläche mit Bronze-
scharnieren angebrachten Beine herausdrehen. An beiden
Enden der schmalen Fläche befinden sich eingelassene
Messing aschenbecher.
H. 65/69, L. 145, B. 52 cm
Privatsammlung, Paris

30 Schreibtisch (MB1055), um 1926
Sykomore
Rechteckige Arbeitsfläche mit schräg abfallenden Seiten-
flächen. Beim Aufschieben der Seitenflächen kommen
flache Behälter zum Vorschein.
H. 69, B. 125, T. 50 cm
Privatsammlung, Paris

31 Toilettentisch (MB1009), 1926/27
Nußbaum
Niedrige, J-förmige Tischfläche auf einer Stütze mit drei
Schubladen auf der linken, gerade Stütze aus Massivholz
auf der rechten Seite

H. 53,5, B. 95, T. 74,5 cm
Privatsammlung, Paris

32 Schreibtisch (MB673), um 1927
Palisander und Schmiedeeisen
L-förmige Arbeitsfläche, eingefaßt in Schmiedeeisen. Auf
der rechten Seite bilden die Verlängerungen der schmiedeeisernen Beine die Stütze für ein rechteckiges Brett
über der Arbeitsfläche, an dem auch ein kleines Schränk-
chen aufgehängt ist. Auf der linken Seite befindet sich ein
freitragendes, drehbares Telefonbord
H. 83,5, B. 161,5, T. 103,5 cm
Privatsammlung, Paris

33 Hocker (SN3), um 1927
Palisander oder Mahagoni mit Metall oder Schmiedeeisen
Sitz aus Holz mit Stützen aus Metall
H. 46/49, B. 49, T. 38 cm
Privatsammlung, Paris

**34 Toilettentisch und Hocker, Ensemble, (MS423 &
MT1015), um 1926/27**
Sykomore und versilbertes Metall
Rechteckige Platte mit leicht eingelassener Mitte und bo-
genförmiger Vorderseite. Seitenstützen aus Massivholz.
Schräg abfallender Spiegel mit verstellbarer Beleuchtungs-
installation, so daß wahlweise der Spiegel oder der Benut-
zer des Spiegels beleuchtet wird. Hocker aus Sykomore
(siehe auch 26 Stuhl (MT1015), um 1923)
Maße unbekannt
Galerie Doria, Paris

**35 Toilettentisch mit Kosmetikschrank (MS418),
um 1927**
Sykomore und Schmiedeeisen
Bestehend aus zwei um ein Gelenk drehbaren Elementen,
einem Ganzfigurspiegel mit Holzrahmen auf der rechten,
einem Schrank mit fester Tischplatte und drehbarem Bord
auf der linken Seite. Die beiden einzeln mit Schmiedeeisen
umrahmten Elemente stehen auf drei schmiedeeisernen
Beinen.
H. 166/116, B. 66/95, T. 9/30 cm
Sammlung Musée d'Art Moderne de Ville de Paris, Paris

36 Bürotisch (MT876), um 1929
Metall und mit rotem Leder überzogenes Holz
Tisch für Schreib- und Rechenmaschinen, bestehend aus
zwei Elementen: rechts eine unbewegliche, rechteckige
Fläche mit Seitenstütze, die ein Metallschränkchen mit ge-
wölbter, nach unten zu öffnender Tür trägt; links eine
schwenkbare Arbeitsfläche auf schmiedeeisernen Stützen
H. 60, B. 155, T. 40 cm
Privatsammlung, Paris

37 Wäschetruhe (MA373), um 1927
Außen Augennußbaum, innen Sykomore
Die Kastenkommode wird auf drei Seiten von langen,
schmalen Schmiedeeisenstücken getragen. Enthält drei
Fachböden und acht Schubladen auf der einen Seite, fünf-
zehn kleine Fächer und fünf flache Schubladen auf der
anderen Seite.
H. 99, B. 70, T. 40 cm
Privatsammlung, Paris

38 Schrank, um 1923
Eiche
Garderobe, bestehend aus drei Einzelfüllung-Türen und
vier Schubladen auf vier kugelförmigen Füßen
H. 148, B. 158, T. 48 cm
Privatsammlung, Paris

39 Niedriger Tisch (MB152), um 1925
Satz aus vier hölzernen, dreieckig gestalteten Tischen, von
einer einzelnen Stütze aus schwenkbar. Die Grundfläche
läßt sich als Bücherschrank benutzen.
Gesamthöhe 81, Tisch H. 56,5, B. 61, T. 37,5, 31, 29
und 26 cm
Galerie Vallois, Paris

40 Kaminsessel (MF313), um 1926
Velours, Gobelin oder Leder
Die Polsterrückenlehne ist zu einer Seite hin schmaler
H. 57, B. 90 cm
Privatsammlung, Paris

41 Stuhl (MF276), um 1924
Nußbaum, Sykomore, Palisander, Eiche oder gebeizte
Buche, und Sitz aus Leder oder Stoff

Nach hinten gewölbte, senkrechte Rückenlehne, ver-
jüngte Beine aus Sykomore, Sitz mit Stoff bezogen
H. 86, B. 52, T. 42 cm
Privatsammlung, Paris

42 Barhocker (MT344), 1926
Holz und Metall
Konkav geformter Sitz aus Massivholz auf Stahlrohrbei-
nen, die auf runden Holzfüßen stehen
H. 88, Sitz 35 × 35 cm
Galerie Arc en Seine, Paris

43 Spieltisch, um 1928
Holz und Metall
Quadratische Tischplatte mit abgerundeten Ecken. Die fla-
chen Holzplatten mit einer Vertiefung für Gläser oder
Aschenbecher bilden beim Herausziehen auf allen Seiten
eine Diagonale. Die Tischplatte steht auf Beinen aus Me-
tallrohr mit runden Füßen, gebogte Metallverstrebungen
bilden Bögen zwischen diesen Beinen.
H. 73, Tischplatte 79 × 79 cm
Galerie Doria, Paris

44 Tisch, um 1927
Stabiles Holz und Schmiedeeisen
Rechteckige, abgekantete Tischplatte aus Massivholz auf
schmiedeeisernen Beinen, deren Enden durch eine Quer-
stange aus Metall verbunden sind, die auf Metallkugeln
ruht. Dadurch läßt sich der Tisch leicht verschieben.
H. 47,5, L. 120, B. 70 cm
Galerie Vallois, Paris

45 Stuhl (MC767), um 1927
Metall und Geflecht
Metallgerahmte, gerade Rückenlehne mit ebenfalls ge-
rahmten, konvex gestaltetem Sitz, beides aus Geflecht.
Der Stuhl steht auf dünnen Metallstützen, eingerahmt in
dünne Stützen aus Metall
H. 80, B. 35, T. 55 cm
Privatsammlung, Paris

46 Niedriger Rohr- und Glastisch, um 1932
Duraluminiumrohr und Glas
Zwei Tischplatten auf Duraluminiumrohrgestell. Die Rohre
sind so gebogen und verschweißt, daß sie unten ein T
bilden. Die große, halbrunde Glasplatte ist mit drei Beinen
verschraubt, die kleine, halbrunde Glasplatte stützt sich
auf zwei angeschweißte Träger.
H. 60, B. 62, T. 63
Stärke der Glasplatte: 2,1 cm
Privatsammlung, Paris

Remerciements

L'auteur tient à exprimer sa profonde recon-
naissance à toute la famille Dalsace-Vellay pour
la constante générosité, les encouragements et
la patience dont elle a fait preuve durant la pré-
paration de ce livre, et en particulier à Marc
Vellay dont le travail original sur Chareau demeure la plus importante source d'information
relative au designer. J'exprime tout spécialement ma gratitude à Bernard Bauchet, mon ancien étudiant, et à Inigo Fernandez de Castro,
qui ont tous deux partagé avec moi les fruits de
leurs recherches et de leurs réflexions. Les familles Brunschwig et Fahri, Madame Dufau et
Olivier Dufau m'ont apporté leur généreux sou-
tien, de même que M. François Halard et M.
Pierre Vago. Les responsables des archives
consacrées à Chareau au Museum of Modern
Art, New York, et au Musée des Arts Décoratifs, Paris, et les galeries Denis Doria et Arc-en-
Seine m'ont été d'un grand secours. Pour finir,
je tiens à remercier l'Association des Amis de la
Maison de Verre pour les nombreuses idées et
critiques qu'elle m'a soumises au cours de mon
travail.
La maison d'édition remercie tout particulièrement les photographes Jordi Sarrà et Jacques
Vasseur pour les photos en couleurs des meubles de Chareau et de la Maison de Verre. Nous
remercions également les photographes et archives suivant: Archives de l'Association des
Amis de la Maison de Verre; Archives de la Ville
de Paris/F. Abdourahim; Thérèse Bonney;
CIAM-Archiv, Institut für Geschichte und Theorie der Architektur der Eidgenössischen Technischen Hochschule, Zurich; Jean Collas;
Mme. Pierre Dufau; Peter Feierabend; Galerie Arc-en-Seine, Paris; Galerie Doria, Paris; Galerie Félix Marcilhac, Paris; Galerie Vallois, Paris;
François Halard; Evelyn Hofer, New York; André Kertész; Musée d'Art Moderne de la Ville
de Paris, Paris; Musée des Arts Décoratifs, Paris; M. Routhier, Studio Lourmel, Paris;
S.A.D.G., Paris; Brian Brace Taylor; G. Thiriet;
M. Zuber.

Acknowledgements

The author wishes to express his profound
thanks to the entire Dalsace-Vellay family for
their constant generosity, encouragement and
patience in the preparation of this book, and
especially to Marc Vellay whose pioneering
work on Chareau remains the most important
source of information on the designer. To Bernard Bauchet, my former student, and to Inigo
Fernandez de Castro, who both shared their research and reflections with me, goes special
gratitude. The Brunschwig and Fahri families,
Madame Pierre Dufau and Olivier Dufau were
particularly generous, as was Mr François
Halard and Mr Pierre Vago. Those reponsible
for the Chareau archival material at The
Museum of Modern Art in New York and the
Musée des Arts Décoratifs in Paris, and the Gal-
leries Denis Doria and Arc-en-Seine, were most
helpful. Finally, I wish to acknowledge the
many insights and criticisms offered by the
Association des Amis de la Maison de Verre in
the course of my work.
The publishers would like to extend particular
thanks to the photographers Jordi Sarrà and
Jacques Vasseur for the colour photographs of
Chareau's furniture and of the Maison de Verre.
We also thank the following photographers and
archives: Archives de l'Association des Amis
de la Maison de Verre; Archives de la Ville de
Paris/F. Abdourahim; Thérèse Bonney; CIAM-
Archiv, Institut für Geschichte und Theorie der
Architektur der Eidgenössischen Technischen
Hochschule, Zurich; Jean Collas; Mme. Pierre
Dufau; Peter Feierabend; Galerie Arc-en-Seine,
Paris; Galerie Doria, Paris; Galerie Félix Mar-
cilhac, Paris; Galerie Vallois, Paris; François
Halard; Evelyn Hofer, New York; André Ker-
tész; Musée d'Art Moderne de la Ville de Paris,
Paris; Musée des Arts Décoratifs, Paris;
M. Routhier, Studio Lourmel, Paris; S.A.D.G.,
Paris; Brian Brace Taylor; G. Thiriet; M. Zuber.

Danksagung

Der ausdrückliche Dank des Autors geht an die
gesamte Familie Dalsace-Vellay für ihre großzü-
gige Unterstützung und Geduld bei den Vorbe-
reitungen zu diesem Buch und besonders an
Marc Vellay, dessen Pionierarbeit über Chareau
meine wichtigste Informationsquelle geblieben
ist. Mein besonderer Dank gilt Bernard
Bauchet, meinem früheren Studenten, und
Inigo Fernandez de Castro, die mich beide an
ihren Untersuchungen und Überlegungen teil-
haben ließen. Die Familien Brunschwig und
Fahri, Frau Pierre Dufau und Olivier Dufau
ebenso Herr François Halard und Herr Pierre
Vago haben wesentlichen Anteil am Zustande-
kommen dieses Buches. Die Mitarbeiter des
Museum of Modern Art in New York und des
Musée des Art Décoratifs in Paris, die mir das
Archivmaterial über Chareau zur Verfügung
stellten, waren mir bei meiner Arbeit überaus
behilflich. Zum Abschluß möchte ich der Association des Amis de la Maison de Verre für die
vielen Einblicke und kritischen Beurteilungen
danken, die sie mir im Lauf meiner Arbeit bot.
Der besondere Dank des Verlages gilt den Fotografen Jordi Sarrà und Jacques Vasseur für die
Farbfotografien der Möbel Chareaus sowie der
Maison de Verre. Weiterhin danken wir den fol-
genden Fotografen und Archiven: Archives de
l'Association des Amis de la Maison de Verre;
Archives de la Ville de Paris/F. Abdourahim;
Thérèse Bonney; CIAM-Archiv, Institut für Ge-
schichte und Theorie der Architektur der Eidge-
nössischen Technischen Hochschule, Zürich;
Jean Collas; Mme. Pierre Dufau; Peter Feier-
abend; Galerie Arc-en-Seine, Paris; Galerie Do-
ria, Paris; Galerie Félix Marcilhac, Paris; Galerie
Vallois, Paris; François Halard; Evelyn Hofer,
New York; André Kertész; Musée d'Art Mo-
derne de la Ville de Paris, Paris; Musée des Arts
Décoratifs, Paris; M. Routhier, Studio Lourmel,
Paris; S.A.D.G., Paris; Brian Brace Taylor;
G. Thiriet; M. Zuber.